Economic segregation in England

Economic segregation in England

Causes, consequences and policy

Geoffrey Meen, Kenneth Gibb, Jennifer Goody, Thomas McGrath
and Jane Mackinnon

JOSEPH ROWNTREE
FOUNDATION

First published in Great Britain in December 2005 by

The Policy Press
Fourth Floor, Beacon House
Queen's Road
Bristol BS8 1QU
UK

Tel no   +44 (0)117 331 4054
Fax no   +44 (0)117 331 4093
E-mail   tpp-info@bristol.ac.uk
www.policypress.org.uk

Published for the Joseph Rowntree Foundation by The Policy Press

ISBN 1 86134 813 4

British Library Cataloguing in Publication Data
A catalogue record for this report is available from the British Library.

Library of Congress Cataloging-in-Publication Data
A catalog record for this report has been requested.

Geoffrey Meen is Professor of Applied Economics at The University of Reading, UK. **Kenneth Gibb** is Reader and Head of the Department of Urban Studies at the University of Glasgow, UK. **Jennifer Goody** is a management consultant and partner in the Peter Brown Partnership, UK, specialising in data analysis. **Thomas McGrath** is a research officer at the University of Reading. **Jane Mackinnon** is a research associate at Glasgow University.

The **Joseph Rowntree Foundation** has supported this project as part of its programme of research and innovative development projects, which it hopes will be of value to policy makers, practitioners and service users. The facts presented and views expressed in this report are, however, those of the authors and not necessarily those of the Foundation.

Cover design by Qube Design Associates, Bristol.
Printed in Great Britain by Hobbs the Printers, Southampton.

Contents

List of figures and tables

Figures

Tables

Acknowledgements

The authors would like to thank the members of the Advisory Group, established by the Joseph Rowntree Foundation, for their valuable contributions to our project. The Advisory Group consisted of Glen Bramley, Paul Cheshire, Annie Grist, Michael Kell, Katharine Knox and Theresa McDonagh.

Introduction

In January 2005, the Office of the Deputy Prime Minister (ODPM) unveiled its Five-Year Plans for housing and for neighbourhood revitalisation in two companion documents, *Sustainable Communities: Homes for All* and *Sustainable Communities: People, Places and Prosperity* (ODPM 2005a, 2005b). The first of these includes proposals for an expansion of home-ownership for low and medium-income households[1]. Key objectives in the second include:

> Faster progress to narrow the gap between the best and worst off to make sure opportunity and choice are for all, including a new more radical approach to renewal in a small number of very disadvantaged areas with the aim to create neighbourhoods with a more sustainable mix of tenures and incomes and address the problems of worklessness, skills, crime, poor environments and poor health. (ODPM News Release, 2005/0021)

Although this report has comments to make on home ownership, its primary emphasis is on the issues raised in the quotation. In particular, it concentrates on attempts to achieve a more balanced mix of tenures and incomes. This has been accepted, almost without question, as a key objective in successive government documents as a way of reducing poverty and improving social justice, although the academic literature has expressed reservations about what can be achieved by such measures.

However, even if integrated neighbourhoods are desirable, there are major impediments to their achievement. One of our concerns is that segregated communities are, in some sense, 'natural' outcomes, even if everyone agrees that integration is desirable. Therefore, policy is attempting to counteract deep-seated trends. Certainly the patterns of segregation that are described in this report provide little evidence that policy has managed to reduce segregation over the past 20 years.

However, description is not enough. Research is needed to understand and quantify the underlying processes that lead to the observed spatial patterns and can identify the policy instruments that are most likely to be successful. Currently, the necessary models that can help us are almost entirely lacking in the economics literature. This problem was recognised at the time of the publication of the Urban White Paper (see Robson et al, 2000). This report is an attempt to begin to close the gap.

Although residential location theory has provided major insights into the spatial structure of cities over the years, our view is that this approach is insufficient to explain the *dynamic* processes of change over time. Therefore, the main development of this report is to provide an empirical analysis of the dynamic processes that lead to the observed patterns of economic segregation. From this, areas most at risk can be identified and policy recommendations drawn. However, an important conclusion of our work is that there is no panacea. One-size-fits-all solutions are inappropriate.

---

[1] An expansion in owner-occupation to these groups also forms an important element of US housing policy. One of the reasons for this emphasis arises from the potential social capital and externalities generated by ownership.

Policies that work in one area may not work in others; technically, this is because of the non-linearity in the economic and social systems of neighbourhoods. Government policies for the Pathfinder Renewal Areas hint that the problem has already been recognised, even without the formal economic analysis. Furthermore, the Five-Year Plan is testing radical and intensive approaches to renewal in three particularly disadvantaged estates in Harpurhey in Manchester, Gipton in Leeds and Canning Town in Newham[2]. Each of these measures recognises that conventional approaches are not appropriate in the most disadvantaged areas; this is an example of non-linearity. However, this also means that conventional analysis used for national and regional economic systems is inappropriate and our report presents novel approaches to the modelling of local economic systems.

Observed patterns of integration and segregation are the outcome of the changing location choices and constraints faced by individual households. The availability of suitable housing provides one constraint, but more general economic and neighbourhood conditions are of equal if not more importance. Low-income households tend to be trapped in the worst locations, whereas high-income households can escape more easily. Polarisation ensues. Indeed, it has been argued that segregation is not in fact a spatial problem at all. The most deprived and segregated communities are simply the areas in which those with the lowest skills are forced to live. Even if there is evidence that 'place' has an effect, clearly skills-based policies work alongside area-based initiatives – they are not alternatives. The analysis in this report, therefore, is consistent with models of cumulative causation identified in the work of Power and Mumford (1999), for example. As in the quotation from *Sustainable Communities: People, Places and Prosperity* printed at the beginning of this chapter, worklessness, skills, crime, poor environments and poor health and all interrelated and build upon each other. All of this implies that moving and migration processes are of central importance in explaining segregation and this report spends a considerable amount of effort in modelling the patterns. An important finding is that local moving patterns can be destabilising for an area and, hence, contribute to segregation.

The models in this report concentrate primarily on supply-side influences on behaviour. It could be argued that insufficient attention is paid to the role of changing patterns of demand for different economic goods across the country. In fact, patterns of deprivation and segregation are heavily dependent on the national and regional contexts. The long-run decline in production away from heavy industry and manufacturing clearly has an effect on levels of deprivation (although not necessarily segregation), contributing to the North–South divide. As a result, different regions suffer from different housing problems. Areas of low demand, for example, are predominantly in the North and Midlands and, consequently, the Pathfinder Areas are in these regions. However, patterns of poverty and deprivation have never been that simple. London possesses some of the most deprived local authorities in the country and, more generally, at a time of national and regional economic expansion, some local areas remain immune to the gains. All local areas do not expand at the same rate. Therefore, this report attempts to abstract from national and regional demand trends and tries to isolate the different local patterns within these areas. Nevertheless, it does recognise that different policies are often required for different areas, depending on the wider regional context.

Our conclusions come from three pieces of empirical evidence. The first is a modelling exercise, conducted at the local authority and ward level, which explains house prices, deprivation, incomes, employment status and migration. The equations are programmed into a simulation model in order to explain how patterns of segregation arise. Although, strictly, the spatial delineations do not conform to neighbourhoods, they are the finest spatial levels, in our view, reasonable statistical models can be constructed. The work, however, is aided by the much-improved neighbourhood indicators now available and the models are the first to be constructed at this spatial level. The models are enhanced by complementary analysis conducted at Output Areas and Super Output Areas – the finest spatial areas defined for the 2001 Census. As noted earlier in this chapter, migration and moving are central to explaining the patterns; however, there are limits to what

---

[2] The scheme was extended to six more areas in the 2005 Budget.

can be explained by aggregate data. In particular, we want to know what are the key factors that influence decisions to move to particular areas. Is it the quality of local schools, the sporting or cultural facilities or absence of crime, or what? If the relative importance of each can be quantified, an indicator is obtained of where resources should be concentrated. Therefore, the second piece of empirical work uses individual data from the British Household Panel Survey to look at location decisions. The two pieces of work together allow us to obtain a fuller picture of the factors affecting segregation. The third piece of evidence comes from three case studies. Our worry is that, although policy may attempt to promote mixed communities by building social housing in predominantly owner-occupied areas and vice versa, the extent to which mixing is maintained over time is not clear. Currently, there is little evidence on this key aspect and the case studies are designed to shed light by tracing the development of the estates over the past 10 years. Although case studies can never lead to general conclusions, we attempt to test hypotheses about which developments are likely to be most successful.

In summary, this report asks:

- What do we mean by economic segregation? What is the difference between deprivation, sustainability and segregation?
- How has the spatial pattern of segregation changed over time?
- Are mixed communities unambiguously desirable or are there limits to what can be achieved by such policies?
- Why is it so difficult to achieve mixed communities?
- What policies, if any, are likely to be most successful in reducing segregation?

Chapter 2 of this report is concerned primarily with defining the underlying concepts. For example, how should segregation be measured? Chapter 3 considers the literature on mixed communities, which is of relevance to later chapters. Chapter 4 presents descriptive evidence on the changing patterns of segregation in England over the last three censuses. Chapter 5 presents the empirical evidence on the dynamics of local housing market. Chapter 6 considers migration and moving decisions, both of which generate the observed processes of segregation. In Chapter 7, the results are brought together in a simulation model. Chapter 8 presents supporting evidence from the case studies. Finally, Chapter 9 brings the results together and draws conclusions on the efficacy of different policies in achieving mixed communities.

2

Concepts and methods

This chapter clarifies some of the concepts and methods to be used later in the report, since confusion is evident in some of the current policy debate. The key distinctions to be brought out are:

- the difference between deprivation and segregation;
- the relationship between segregation, sustainability and stability;
- definitions of mixed communities in terms of ethnicity, income, tenure, labour market status, or other indicator;
- the different ways in which segregation can be measured; and
- the appropriate spatial dimensions for analysis.

Deprivation versus segregation

Although the report has quite a lot to say about both deprivation and segregation, they are not the same concept. For example, a local authority may exhibit a high score on the Index of Multiple Deprivation (IMD), but this represents an average across the local authority. Segregation refers to the distribution of deprivation within the local authority (or other spatial entity), perhaps across the wards. The indices of segregation used here attempt to capture aspects of the distribution. The well-known Dissimilarity Index, for example, measures the extent to which minority groups would have to move between wards to obtain an equal distribution of the minority group across the local authority. It does not necessarily follow, therefore, that high average levels of deprivation in the local authorities are closely related to high levels of segregation. In an extreme case, *all* the wards of a given local authority could have a high level of deprivation, in which case there would be no segregation. There is an important policy reason for considering the dispersion of deprivation within a local authority as well as the average level. Local authorities comprise a unit of government, but, as we shall see later, typically few local authorities as a whole have very high levels of deprivation; they comprise a combination of areas of high and low deprivation. As Beroube (2005) points out, if progress in reducing deprivation is purely in terms of the better off neighbourhoods, the strategy is not succeeding.

In summary, examining changes in spatial deprivation is important, but does not tell the full story.

Segregation, sustainability and stability

At first sight, it might appear that mixed communities are both sustainable and stable. In fact, there is no necessary reason why this should be the case. An important part of the literature suggests that segregated communities are the 'natural' stable state.

Sustainability is one of the most commonly used buzzwords in policy debate. However, the term is not always precisely defined[1]. In the *Sustainable Communities Plan* (ODPM, 2003), for example, 'key requirements for sustainable communities' are listed, but these do not constitute a definition. However, the Egan Review (which considers the adequacy of key skills for delivering the aims of the *Sustainable Communities Plan*) (Egan, 2004, p 7), recommends a working definition of sustainability, derived from the requirements of the Plan:

> [S]ustainable communities meet the diverse needs of existing and future residents, their children and other users, contribute to a high quality of life and provide opportunity and choice. They achieve this in ways that make effective use of natural resources, enhance the environment, promote social cohesion and inclusion and strengthen economic prosperity.

The definition is used to identify seven elements of a sustainable community, backed up by fifty indicators that could be used to monitor progress towards the goals over time. These include subjective indicators of residents' happiness combined with more objective measures such as deprivation index rankings, crime rates and house prices. Some of these indicators are used in our quantitative work later. A similar definition is used in *Sustainable Communities: People, Places and Prosperity*:

> Sustainable communities are places where people want to live and work, now and in the future. They meet the diverse needs of existing and future residents, are sensitive to their environment, and contribute to a high quality of life. They are safe and inclusive, well planned, built and run, and offer equality of opportunity and good services for all. (p 56)

The key point to note is that, although the definitions suggest that sustainable communities should include social mix, there is no reason why mixed communities should be stable and, therefore, sustainable. Some findings from the theoretical literature on social interactions and dynamics illustrate the point.

An important branch of the recent literature suggests that poverty traps and economic segregation between areas occur because of the existence of the social interactions between the residents of any neighbourhood. Persistent inequality arises because of these interactions. Intuitively, the stronger are the interactions or ties, the more likely are segregated communities and the more difficult it becomes for policy to promote integrated communities. At one level, the point may appear obvious. If ties with local family and friends are very strong, there is a disincentive to move. Most household moves in England are only over very short distances in order to avoid disrupting these ties. There is also anecdotal evidence to suggest that households are not prepared to move away from deprived areas, even if given the opportunity to do so, because they do not wish to lose the support (and sometimes security) provided by their local social networks. Therefore, the stronger are the social interactions, the more difficult it becomes to promote integrated communities and simply providing financial incentives to move may not work.

However, the implications of the theoretical literature are potentially even more devastating for policy. Indeed, in an important forerunner of the literature, Schelling (1971) was concerned with the conditions under which individual residential location decisions interact to produce racially segregated neighbourhoods. A central insight is to demonstrate that, even if everyone wishes to live in mixed (integrated) neighbourhoods, the sum of the individual free choices will, generally, generate segregated communities. Later work by Young (1998) and Krugman (1996) demonstrate that mixed communities are 'stochastically unstable' – small random shocks to an integrated structure lead to a breakdown in the structure and eventually to segregation. Meen and Meen (2002) present some simple simulation models that possess these properties. Furthermore, models in which

---

[1] Alternative concepts are discussed in Meen (2004b).

neighbourhood interactions and peer group pressures are important may exhibit 'tipping', a sudden change from one state to another. Areas, for example, suddenly 'take off'.

In summary, however, there is no necessary reason to believe a priori that sustainable, and stable, communities will be mixed.

Mixed communities

What do we mean by mixed communities? Clearly there are a large number of possible indicators that could be chosen. The traditional concern of the US literature has been with *ethnic* segregation. In the US, Cutler et al (1999) trace racial segregation in major cities from the late 19th century, based on Census figures. In Britain, however, consistent questions on ethnicity do not appear in successive censuses. Based on the 1991 Census, Johnston et al (2002) suggest that segregation of black households in Britain is not as extreme as in the US, but it is not possible to trace *changes* in racial segregation over time on a consistent basis. Our emphasis is on economic rather than ethnic segregation. Of course, the two are not unrelated and 70% of all English ethnic minority residents live within the country's 88 most deprived districts (NRU, 2002).

However, even limiting the study to economic segregation, the choice of indicators is potentially wide. In a comprehensive study of the spatial distribution of poverty in Britain, Green (1994) relies exclusively on Census data, comparing the positions in 1981 and 1991. Green concentrates on the unemployment rate, the percentage of households with no car, percentage of households in rental accommodation, inactivity rates, occupational class percentages and qualifications. However, notice that the most obvious variable – income – is not included in the list, because, in the UK, no income information is included in the Census. This is a major drawback, although Green indicates that there is a high correlation between income and the variables she considers.

The variables considered here are broadly similar to those of Green, since we are also dependent on (2001) Census data and we wish to draw comparisons with the earlier work. In particular, we consider tenure, unemployment and educational performance. Tenure is chosen because of its links to policy; the main instrument to induce mixed communities is through variations in tenure. However, tenure mix is not an objective in itself; it is an instrument, or at least an indirect target, aimed at wider social integration. The distribution of social housing is now a good indicator of deprivation, because it is dominated by low-income households. It would not necessarily have been a good indicator in the immediate post-Second World War era, when public housing was occupied by a much higher percentage of working households. Therefore, tenure is not necessarily an end in itself.

Unemployment is widely used in this study. Unemployment is one of the few indicators that is available regularly on a spatially disaggregated basis, outside the Census. Also, so much of policy has been geared towards 'getting people back to work' and, therefore, the success of this policy, in terms of segregation, can be traced over time. Furthermore, as we shall see, labour market status is the single most important determinant quantitatively of the Index of Multiple Deprivation (IMD). Finally, the simulation model developed later determines local unemployment within its structure and so we can look at possible patterns of segregation that may emerge in the future.

The final set of indicators considered concern education. Again, policy is heavily oriented towards skills improvements and, indeed, our models indicate that skills levels are one of the most important determinants of labour market status.

Measuring segregation

Segregation is a multidimensional concept (see Massey and Denton, 1988), but the most commonly used measure in the literature is the Index of Dissimilarity. We also concentrate on this measure in order to aid comparisons with other work. As noted earlier in this chapter, the index considers the percentage of minorities in any ward (or other spatial entity) relative to the majority percentage. More precisely, the index is a measure of the proportion of a given minority group that would need to move across wards in order to obtain a perfectly even distribution of that group across the city[2]. Of course, the index can be constructed for any of the socioeconomic variables discussed earlier in this chapter, rather than the commonly used ethnicity measure. The value of the index ranges between 0 and 1. Massey and Denton suggest that, for ethnicity, a value of <0.3 is low; between 0.3 and 0.6 is moderate; and >0.6 is high. A value of 0 would imply that every ward has the same percentage of minorities as the city average. A value of 1 implies total segregation, where all of the minority live in certain wards and everyone else lives in other locations. However, these rules of thumb apply primarily to ethnicity-based measures. As Abramson et al (1995) indicate, income-based indicators typically show lower levels of segregation, despite the fact that race and poverty are highly correlated. Abramson et al (1995) calculate an average Dissimilarity Index value across the 100 largest US metropolitan areas in 1990 of 0.36 based on income compared with a value of 0.61 based on race.

Although widely used, as Green (1994) points out, there are problems with the measure. First, the smaller the spatial unit under consideration and the smaller the proportion of the population belonging to the minority group, the larger is the expected value of the index. In Britain, wards are not of equal size and this can distort the findings. Second, the index takes no account of the spatial relationship between the areas. Shuffling the spatial units has no effect on the index. However, 'chequerboard' patterns for minorities across the city clearly have different policy implications from patterns of strong spatial contiguity. Following on from these points, it is by no means clear that wards and cities are the appropriate spatial units of measurement. This is convenient for comparison with earlier British studies but, as argued later in this chapter, it may be better to consider segregation across Travel to Work Areas. In general, this is an example of the 'Modifiable Areal Unit Problem', where artificial spatial patterns may be generated through the use of data based on artificial administrative boundaries.

The spatial unit of analysis

Our work concentrates on local phenomena and, in an ideal world, we would decide on the appropriate areal unit and all the analysis would be conducted at that level. However, we do not live in an ideal world. The analysis is constrained by data availability and different units are used for different parts of the study. The study includes elements from local authorities, wards, Super Output Areas, Output Areas and Travel to Work Areas (TTWAs). However, despite this eclectic approach, the aim is to provide an integrated, consistent story about the operation of local markets. Therefore, work on migration at the local authority level, for example, is integrated with work on wards and, indeed, on individual location choice taken from micro-data sets. However, we have not attempted to define Housing Market Areas across the country using traditional hedonic methods. Even if this were possible, arguably it is not appropriate. For the models that we develop, which look at the interactions between housing and labour markets, TTWAs may be more relevant. However, there is no simple answer to this issue.

---

[2] Dorling and Rees (2003) provide a simple example giving the intuition behind the index.

Non-linearity

Non-linearity is fundamental to the results in this report. The reason is that, under non-linearity, policy changes may have either very little effect or very large effects according to where they take place. This implies that spatial targeting is necessary; the areas where policy is likely to be effective have to be identified. An important example of non-linear behaviour is thresholds (see Figure 3.1 of this report). The idea is that an area has to reach a take-off point before policy has any influence or before private capital is attracted to an area. However, once the threshold has been reached, very large changes in the structure of the area can occur, often very quickly.

Formally, non-linearity refers to the nature of the mathematical relationship between two (or more) variables. In the opposite linear case, the relationship is a straight line. Therefore a rise in one variable is associated with a proportionate increase or decrease in the second variable. This relationship is the same for all values of the variables. Therefore, an increase in public expenditure in the wealthy London borough of Richmond, for example, would have the same effect as a rise in deprived Harpurhey in Manchester. Consequently: (a) there is no need to identify areas where policy is most effective (all areas have the same responsiveness); and (b) the effectiveness of the policy is proportionate to the size of the expenditure. Hence, a series of small expenditures has the same effect as one large expenditure of the same amount. Neither of these properties occurs if responses are non-linear.

3

Are mixed communities desirable? The poverty of place

Some results from the literature

The purpose here is not to review the literature comprehensively, but rather to use key references to identify and illuminate important questions for the research. A broader review can be found in Beroube (2005). There is both a long-standing academic interest and a contemporary policy focus on constructing and sustaining mixed communities (Parkinson, 1998). As noted in Chapter 1, the government strongly supports community-level renewal on these lines and the Joseph Rowntree Foundation (JRF) has funded research and supported initiatives in this area emphasising tenure diversification, income and social mix within local communities.

Kleinhans (2004) shows that the UK has pursued these diversification policies for more than 20 years and that it has been explicit in much urban regeneration since the early 1990s (see also Kintrea et al, 1996; Tunstall, 2003). Repeatedly, both the former Conservative and current Labour governments have identified mixed tenure communities as policy goals to help turn around and sustain local communities (for example, DETR, 2000). Kleinhans argues that this policy discourse is often underdeveloped: clear goals, concepts and indicators are not always set or defined, the complexity of these processes is not sufficiently appreciated, and the relevant spatial scale is often left unclear.

Martin and Watkinson (2003) investigated the impact of mixed tenure initiatives on social housing estates for the JRF. They surveyed 72 larger housing associations and 78 local authorities. The research found that there is in fact a greater amount of mixed tenure work introducing forms of home ownership into social housing areas than is perhaps widely realised. Although this had primarily been to achieve financial aims, respondents claimed important social and financial benefits of mixed tenure: lower turnover and higher tenant stability, higher levels of demand and area reputation, as well as a more balanced household mix and increased property values. Martin and Watkinson (2003, p 4) argue that, while much of the prior debate had been concerned with the extent to which mixed-income communities achieve socially inclusive networks or whether neighbours develop common interests, new research indicates practical benefits such as contentment among households and social stability.

Kleinhans (2004) summarises the key evidence from the literature:

- There is consensus that tenure diversification leads to improvements in the physical characteristics of homes and neighbourhoods.
- There is evidence that insertion of owners has an indirect positive effect on areas through the behaviour of owners, independently of the characteristics of renters. In particular, their increased emphasis on maintenance and on the outlook of their immediate neighbourhood is argued to spill over to everyone's benefit.

- There is some evidence that diversification may enhance the likelihood and effectiveness of collective action at the community level, and this may be linked to evidence that such policies do indeed reduce stigmatisation and enhance area reputation.
- UK authors in particular support more 'pepper potting' of tenure because of the evidence that neighbourhoods remain or become more segmented despite tenure diversification policies (echoing the themes of this project and evidence within the New Town context of Peterborough, discussed in Chapter 8 of this report).
- There is evidence, however, that social mix is in fact a relatively insignificant explanation of neighbourhood satisfaction; that is, it is more to do with environmental quality, privacy, perceived safety, and so on.

Atkinson and Kintrea (2000) examine new owner-occupied markets in disadvantaged Scottish communities. They report that the literature suggests, in general, that introducing home ownership into relatively deprived areas should alter the social mix, increase social stability and help foster stronger communities (in terms of self-reliance, sustainability, and so on). Atkinson and Kintrea review the theory and evidence on social mix. Social mix is an old idea at least going back to 19th-century social reform and re-emerging in several guises, not least the New Towns (see our case study in Peterborough):

> However, commentators are generally sceptical about the extent to which social mix can be achieved by policy action because communities are socially constructed. (Atkinson and Kintrea, 2000, p 96)

Can policy makers actually influence the direction of these complex processes of conflict, exchange and interdependency? Moreover, there is an assumption that residents look in towards their neighbourhood rather than use it as a base for a more outward-looking life.

Wilson (1987) argues that the middle class acts as a social buffer to prevent the more disadvantaged being socially isolated or excluded. They also act to provide sanctions against aberrant behaviour (Atkinson and Kintrea, 2000, p 95). However, Kleinhans (2004) argues that there has been no effective test in the literature of Wilson's argument. Friedrichs (1996) concludes that non-mixed low-income households will be more likely to be spatially and socially isolated.

Atkinson and Kintrea explore the importance of the social networks that spring from weak ties (Granovetter, 1972) relative to strong ties, which tend to be more bounded and actually reduce information sharing beyond the immediate group. Thus, it can be argued that wider social networks might arise from mixed tenure and mixed income communities (see also, Montgomery, 1994). Atkinson and Kintrea (2000, p 96) contend that the notion that neighbourhoods are an important basis or location for social interaction may be anachronistic and that life may be more private and home-centred than hitherto (see also Crow and Allan, 1994). The implication is that the social or neighbourhood impacts of mixing through housing policies may be overstated. Kleinhans (2004, p 377) puts it well:

> [T]he neighbourhood has a diminished, but nonetheless specific, social importance.

Atkinson and Kintrea's review (2000, p 97) concludes that, while bringing wealthier owners into relatively disadvantaged communities may widen social realms, it is less likely to bring different types of people into contact because relationships in communities are no longer the high-level interactions that they once have been, suggesting a 'contradiction between the policy and the evidence about how local communities work'. Their own original research is more positive, although it suggests that one should not make over-optimistic or indeed patronising claims about the insertion of home ownership into social housing communities.

Kleinhans (2004, p 368) examines the social implications of housing diversification. He starts from the assumed consequences of such diversification: a better-working housing market, improved reputation, and positive outcomes with regard to cohesion, inclusion and community participation exemplified by higher levels of local support for neighbourhood facilities and lower maintenance costs. A simple model of this assumed process is set out (Kleinhans, 2004, p 374) where physical housing diversification is believed to lead on to positive population changes (that is social mix, balance and cohesion) and the avoidance of negative population changes (selective out-migration of the upwardly mobile) and this in turn leads to beneficial social implications (for example, improved area reputation, social and visual interaction, positive role models).

Kleinhans (2004, p 378) concludes that the little social interaction between owners and tenants is not surprising since tenure is not the single cause of cross-tenure interaction. Lifestyle and socioeconomic characteristics are important determinants. Beyond this, Kleinhans reaches four important conclusions for this project. First, there is a limited interaction between owners and tenants because of diverging lifestyles and different socioeconomic characteristics. Second, cross-tenure social distances are evident in resident opinions about diversification, for instance, residents favour social mix generally but often do not want different tenures in their area, particularly if the area is dominated by home ownership. Third, the positive behavioural changes that policy makers want to see when diversifying low-income areas can be limited by social processes that inhibit positive effects. Fourth, whereas the social implications of tenure diversification question its effectiveness, it is also of course the case that such policies are championed because they restructure the housing market and provide opportunities for housing career mobility. Such policies are strongly redistributional (and often not in favour of low incomes) but their legitimacy has not been challenged.

In a recent study for the Joseph Rowntree Foundation, Allen et al (2005), reviewed case studies of mixed tenure development 20 years on. Their focus was on purposive mixed tenure planning and children and family experiences of mixing. Each of their case studies was successful in that they remained relatively desirable and contained a relatively limited social range of residents. Residents perceived themselves as ordinary and there was evidence that similarities in housing design helped to mask tenure differences. However, renters and owners lived in different social worlds with limited interaction. There does seem to be evidence of Granovetter's weak social ties in operation, for example, among neighbours and families with school children. The local planned environment, among other factors of which mixed tenure was only one, helped explain the relative stability and success of the case study areas. They conclude that the claims made of mixed tenure are probably exaggerated, for instance, it is no bulwark against broader polarising social trends. In particular, they stress that there was little or no evidence that mixed tenure induced 'role model' or 'bridging social capital' effects (Allen et al, 2005, p 11). They also found that there could be a case made for either pepper-potted or segmented approaches to mixed tenure, provided there is comprehensive planning, high quality residential environments and the blurring of tenure distinctions in housing designs.

This clear dissonance between the academic commentator and the beliefs of policy makers surrounding the pursuit of social and tenure mix raises important questions about the aims of policy and about the evidence base of their effectiveness:

- What is beneficial about mixed neighbourhoods and why is it useful to change neighbourhoods from single to mixed tenure or from undiversified to more varied income levels? In short, why is it important to reduce spatial economic segregation?
- What are the processes that bring about segregation and how do mixed community policies tackle these processes?
- Under what conditions, if any, are mixed communities, once established, sustainable? How important are external drivers relative to internal processes and household behaviour?

- Are there important differences where the form of mixing is by inserting private housing into social housing or where the mixing is in the other direction? Is there evidence that certain types of policy are more effective than others?

Economic efficiency, thresholds and social interactions

Controversy also surrounds the *economic* benefits of mixed communities. The case rests on the view that:

1. Place has an effect on behaviour and outcomes independently of individual circumstances. Therefore, moving low-income households to other areas or 'importing' relatively wealthy households will improve economic opportunities for the low skilled. In the US, the Moving to Opportunity (MTO) programme is an example of the former and the Nehemiah Housing Opportunity Grants Program (NHOP) is an example of the latter (see Cummings et al, 2002). However, the alternative view is that 'place' is simply the location where the low skilled are constrained to live. Therefore, by skills improvement programmes, individuals will be able to raise themselves up and leave the worst locations.
2. Social interactions between individuals in a neighbourhood have an important impact on economic performance. For example, peer group pressures among adolescent males might contribute to poor educational performance with subsequent consequences for job prospects. Similar pressures also change social norms, leading to a rise in crime rates, drug use and higher rates of out-of-wedlock births. Therefore, breaking up such concentrations may contribute to welfare improvements, although peer group effects can, of course, be positive as well as negative.
3. Galster (2002) shows that any *efficiency* gains for the economy as a whole from deconcentrating poverty depend on whether the relationship between income and deprivation is linear or non-linear.
4. A related, although distinct, argument is whether the promotion of home ownership, in itself, leads to an improvement in performance. Ownership generates pride in the community through self-interest since any improvement will be reflected in property values. This externality argument for home ownership is often used in the US to support the existence of subsidies to owner-occupiers and an expansion of ownership to lower-income households.

However, a distinction needs to be drawn between the effects of the *physical environment* and the *interactions* between the residents who live in the neighbourhood. The arguments in the previous section indicate that, although mixing generally improves the physical character of the neighbourhood, it does not necessarily encourage social interactions, in which case traditional peer group influences are likely to remain as strong as ever.

As examples, three longitudinal studies produce mixed findings on the role of the *neighbourhood*. Bolster et al (2004) consider the relationship, for the UK, between income growth over a 10-year period and very local neighbourhoods. They find little association between neighbourhood disadvantage and subsequent income growth. Their results support the view that the main sources of low incomes lie in employment and demographics rather than neighbourhood. Internationally, Oreopolous (2003) tracks children from Toronto over a 30-year time horizon to look at their long-run labour market outcomes. He finds that, although the children were subjected to different living conditions and experienced different exposures to crime, neighbourhood plays little role in determining later earnings. Rather, family differences are much more important. However, Kling et al (2005) use US data from the MTO housing voucher scheme to examine the effect of neighbourhood on youth crime. They find gender differences for females, for example, arrests for violent and property crimes are reduced by relocation. However, for males, arrests for violent crimes are reduced, although arrests for property crimes rise.

More generally, in his review of the literature, Beroube (2005) finds that individual and family circumstances have a stronger effect on outcomes than neighbourhood characteristics. However, he does not dismiss the impact of the neighbourhood and argues that policy interventions that change neighbourhood conditions have a greater impact on the life chances of younger children than older children or adults.

The recognition of *social interactions* is a key element of the modelling and policy work in subsequent chapters, because interactions typically imply non-linear behaviour. Although economics has recognised for many years that interdependencies can influence behaviour, recent research in economics has taken a rather different direction. Broadly, the new models demonstrate that the greater the weight attached to the actions of others compared with one's own actions (for example, the greater the importance of peer groups), the more likely is the possibility of the non-linear outcomes discussed in Chapter 2 of this report. When the interactions between households reach some critical point, they have a disproportionate effect. For example, high-income households may not be prepared to move to more deprived areas until networks of similar households have become established in those areas. For these reasons, it is quite possible for areas of wealth to exist close to areas of deprivation. Even Kensington and Chelsea – the most expensive housing market in the country – contains wards of deprivation associated with high concentrations of social housing.

Galster (2002) stresses the importance of thresholds as one form of non-linear behaviour. Neighbourhoods do not start to decline or gentrify until they pass some trigger point. However, once neighbourhoods pass the threshold, their character can very quickly change. Therefore, social interaction models provide a theoretical framework for analysing the aggregate occurrences that we observe in local housing markets, including cumulative decline, low demand areas and the loss of city populations.

In Figure 3.1, as some indicator variable (X) reaches a critical value, the neighbourhood, measured, for example, in terms of local incomes or house prices (Y), suddenly takes off. One of the indicator variables sometimes suggested is the owner-occupation rate. Once the rate reaches a certain point the area becomes ripe for gentrification.

The areas that are most likely to gentrify or decline are those that lie around the threshold, but the identification of these areas is critical. Appropriate policy intervention is also tied up with identifying the thresholds. Relatively small government expenditures in areas that lie around points A and B have large effects on prices or incomes. By contrast, expenditure at locations well below A may have very little effect and other types of policy, for example, wholesale clearance schemes, might be more appropriate. In other words, 'one-size-fits-all' policies do not work where thresholds exist.

Figure 3.1: Thresholds in local housing markets

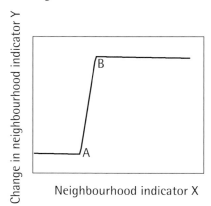

Models of this type also have implications for the economic efficiency (rather than distributional equity) of schemes, such as MTO, designed to move low-income households away from poorer areas. Galster (20002) shows that if the relationship between neighbourhood incomes (vertical axis) and the poverty rate (horizontal axis) in Figure 3.1 is *linear*, there are no efficiency gains (measured in terms of net social benefits) from shifting populations. This arises because the gains to poor households who move to richer areas are offset by the losses to rich households who already lived in those areas. On efficiency grounds, it is insufficient to demonstrate that the incomes of the poor rise on moving. For any gains to occur, the relationship has to be non-linear. Even then, the overall gains only occur if very low poverty neighbourhoods are opened up to the poor. Shifting populations from high poverty areas to moderate poverty areas generates few gains.

Conclusions

- The government has identified mixed tenure communities as policy goals to help turn around and sustain local communities. However, academic analysis is generally sceptical about the extent to which social mix can be achieved by policy.
- Recent JRF research indicated practical benefits such as contentment among households and social stability. There is also wider consensus that tenure diversification leads to positive improvements in the physical characteristics of homes and neighbourhoods. The insertion of owners has an indirect positive effect on areas through the behaviour of owners, independently of the characteristics of renters. Diversification may enhance the likelihood and effectiveness of collective action at the community level, and this may be linked to evidence that such policies do indeed reduce stigmatisation and enhance area reputation.
- There is, however, evidence that social mix is in fact a relatively insignificant explanation of neighbourhood satisfaction; that is, it is more to do with environmental quality, privacy, perceived safety, and so on. The notion that neighbourhoods are an important basis or location for social interaction may be anachronistic. The implication is that the social or neighbourhood impacts of mixing through housing policies may be overstated.
- The little social interaction between owners and tenants is not surprising since tenure is not the single cause of cross-tenure interaction. There is a limited interaction between owners and tenants because of diverging lifestyles and different socioeconomic characteristics. Whereas the social implications of tenure diversification question its effectiveness, it is also the case that such policies are championed because they restructure the housing market and provide opportunities for housing career mobility.
- A full economy analysis of the advantages of social mixing needs to take into account the effect on the existing households in the areas to which the poor move. If the relationship between incomes and neighbourhood poverty is linear, there is *no* advantage to deconcentrating poverty in efficiency terms, although there may still be distributional equity gains.

4

The patterns of segregation in England

This chapter describes (rather than explains) the key patterns of segregation in England, using the three indicator variables – unemployment, tenure and skills. Although concentrating primarily on evidence from the 2001 Census, it also draws on published results from the 1981 and 1991 Censuses in order to provide evidence on the dynamics of change.

Unemployment

Table 4.1 begins by presenting the Dissimilarity Index for the English local authorities, calculated across almost 8,000 wards. More precisely, it presents the 15 top-ranked (most segregated) districts for 2001. First, notice that it does not necessarily follow that the areas of highest unemployment will have the greatest degree of segregation. Hackney in London is one of the most deprived local authorities in the country on the basis of the deprivation index, but has a dissimilarity value of only 0.048, one of the lowest in the country. This reflects the fact that unemployment is almost uniformly high in each of the wards of the local authority. It does not imply an integrated community between rich and poor. In fact, using the Dissimilarity Index, no London borough is high on the rankings[1]. Therefore, we have to be careful in our interpretation. More generally, it does not necessarily follow that high average levels of deprivation in the local authorities are closely related to the indices of segregation[2].

Second, although Cannock Chase tops the list, this is misleading as the outcome arises from its relatively small size and a limited number of outliers with high levels of unemployment. It does not rate highly on other indicators or in earlier studies. By contrast, of the top four ranked wards, Stockton and Middlesbrough, both in the North East of England are more typical. In Stockton, the unemployment rate ranges from 3.0-22.4% and in Middlesbrough 3.8-24.3%. Overall, 11 of the 15 top-ranked local authorities lie in the North of the country (North East, North West, and Yorkshire and Humberside) and none in the South East. The concentration of the highest areas of segregation in the North is even more evident in the map (Figure 4.1).

Third, few, if any, districts have scores above 0.3. The index can vary between values of 0 and 1 and, on the 'rule of thumb' described in Chapter 2 of this report, this might suggest only modest degrees of segregation, but, as noted earlier in this report, the rule of thumb applies primarily to ethnicity and income-related measures typically produce lower scores even in the most deprived areas[3].

---

[1] With the exception of the City of London, which is a special case (see Figure 4.1).
[2] Note that this implies, in our simulation models, that even if they can explain the level of deprivation they do not necessarily explain segregation.
[3] It is shown below that tenure-based measures produce much higher values.

Table 4.1: Indices of dissimilarity (unemployment-based)

Top 15 nationally, local authority districts (LADs) (2001)		
LAD	Region	Index of dissimilarity
Cannock Chase	West Mids	0.304
Stockton-on-Tees	North East	0.284
Middlesbrough	North East	0.270
Preston	North West	0.267
Oldham	North West	0.253
W. Lancs	North West	0.253
Bradford	Yorks & Humber	0.246
Ellesmere Port	North West	0.244
Gloucester	South West	0.236
W. Lindsey	East Mids	0.233
Blyth Valley	North East	0.233
Blackburn	North West	0.232
Crewe	North West	0.231
Derby	East Mids	0.230
Sheffield	Yorks & Humber	0.230

Source: calculated by Suzanne Dixon from the 2001 Census

For policy, however, the question is whether these rankings and, indeed, the absolute levels of the indices have changed over time. The second question is more difficult to answer since the exact definitions of the ward boundaries over which the local authority districts (LADs) indices are constructed have altered over time. Nevertheless, we can still discern patterns in the scores and rankings. As noted earlier, Green (1994) carried out a comprehensive analysis for 1981 and 1991. A broad pattern emerged for 1991. Green found that, in England, Middlesbrough (3), Stockton (2), Preston (4) and West Lancashire (6) were the districts of highest segregation, again all lying in the northern part of Britain. The numbers in brackets are our rankings in 2001[4]. Therefore, the most highly segregated local authorities in 1991 remain high on the 2001 list. In 1991, Middlesbrough yielded a dissimilarity score of 0.31, similar to the values in Table 4.1 despite the ward boundary changes. Furthermore, in terms of changes between 1981 and 1991, Green points to a high degree of continuity in the spatial distributions. All the evidence, therefore, points to the stability of segregation patterns between 1981 and 2001, at least on the unemployment indicator, with the most segregated communities existing in large, older industrial areas. Dorling and Rees (2003) reach similar conclusions. Comparing the four censuses since 1971, they conclude in fact that polarisation has increased. Their analysis uses local authorities (rather than wards), which makes standardisation across censuses slightly easier.

As discussed in Chapter 2 of this report, these results are potentially dependent on the spatial scale of analysis, however. Table 4.1 is calculated for local authorities across the wards in order to aid comparison with earlier work, but, arguably, they should be calculated for Travel to Work Areas (TTWAs) rather than districts. Table 4.2 calculates the index for the sample of TTWAs used in later analysis, again across the wards. These are among the most deprived TTWAs in the country.

---

[4] Oldham was ranked 14 in 1991.

Table 4.2: Indices of dissimilarity (unemployment-based) – Travel to Work Areas (TTWAs)

TTWA	Index of dissimilarity
Birmingham	0.202
Bradford	0.186
Bristol	0.133
Coventry	0.169
Derby	0.201
Dudley and Sandwell	0.137
Hull	0.174
Leeds	0.202
Leicester	0.185
Liverpool	0.168
Manchester	0.179
Middlesbrough and Stockton	0.211
Nottingham	0.204
Sheffield and Rotherham	0.169
Stoke	0.143
Sunderland and Durham	0.133
Tyneside	0.155
Wolverhampton and Walsall	0.156

Table 4.3: Indices of dissimilarity (unemployment-based) – wards

LAD	Ward	Index of dissimilarity
Durham	Shincliffe	0.708
Nottingham	Wollaton East and Lenton Abbey	0.543
Rushcliffe	Tollerton	0.527
Durham	Elvet	0.469
Macclesfield	Gawsworth	0.470
Stafford	Swynnerton	0.446
Newcastle-under-Lyme	Keele	0.436
Newcastle upon Tyne	Moorside	0.422
Blaby	Croft Hill	0.415
Oadby and Wigston	Wigston Meadowcourt	0.401
Durham	St Nicholas	0.391
Gedling	Bestwood Village	0.383
Nottingham	Radford and Park	0.383
Manchester	Fallowfield	0.379
Middlesbrough	Stainton and Thornton	0.378

Alternatively, the index could be calculated over very small spatial units. Table 4.3, therefore, lists the top 15 most segregated wards, calculated over Census Output Areas. Again, all the most segregated areas are in the North and Midlands, but the very high values in some instances demonstrates the problems in dealing with very small scales of analysis. Outliers distort the analysis and too much should not be read into these values.

Figure 4.1: Index of dissimilarity (unemployment-based)

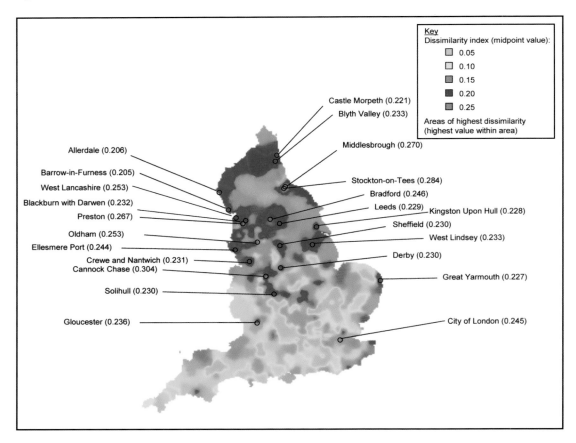

Figure 4.2: Index of dissimilarity (no qualifications)

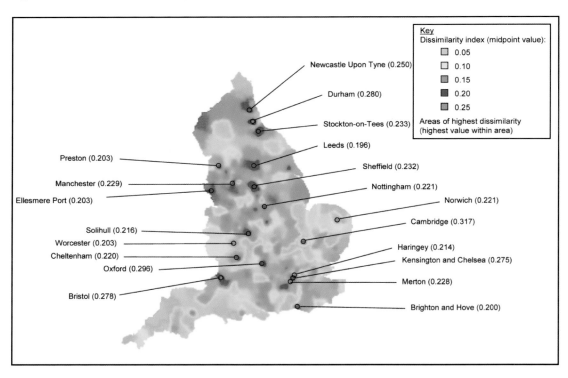

Figure 4.3: Index of dissimilarity (degrees)

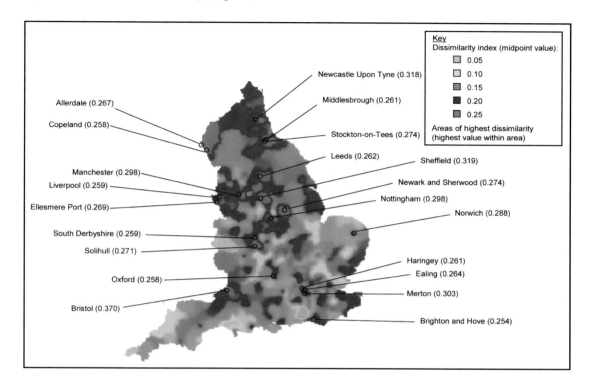

Table 4.4: Indices of dissimilarity (tenure-based)

Region	LAD	Index of dissimilarity
North West	Ellesmere Port	0.523
West Midlands	Solihull	0.460
South East	Portsmouth	0.456
North West	Sefton	0.453
North East	Stockton-on-Tees	0.450
West Midlands	Worcester	0.438
South East	Dartford	0.435
North East	Middlesborough	0.433
North West	Macclesfield	0.432
North West	West Lancashire	0.432
Yorks and Humber	Kingston upon Hull	0.430
South West	Cheltenham	0.427
North West	South Ribble	0.420
North West	Crewe and Nantwich	0.417
North West	Warrington	0.417

Educational attainment

In this case, we examine the distribution of individuals with either no qualifications or with higher education qualifications. Although skills shortages are typically associated with higher unemployment probabilities (see Chapter 7 of this report for evidence), the patterns of segregation are not the same as in Figure 4.1. In fact, areas of high scores are more broadly based, as shown in Figure 4.2. Similarly, there are areas of high segregation scores for those with degrees in the South (Figure 4.3). Perhaps, unsurprisingly, university towns often feature highly on this indicator.

Tenure

Table 4.4 looks at the segregation of those in social housing. The first feature that stands out is that the absolute values are much higher than for the other variables. In Ellesmere Port, more than 50% of households would have to change tenure for an equal distribution of social housing to exist across the wards[5]. Second, the pattern is not a simple North–South divide. Portsmouth stands out in the South. Third, comparisons over time are distorted by Right-to-Buy sales. Nevertheless, Green found that Ellesmere Port was ranked first in 1991 and second in 1981.

Conclusions

In summary:

- Segregation based on unemployment remains heavily concentrated on the older industrial, northern and Midlands areas.
- However, patterns of segregation on the remaining indicators are more complex. It is not a simple issue of a North–South divide. Patterns of segregation depend on which indicator is employed.
- There is little, if any, evidence that the extent of segregation has declined over the past 20 years, although there are difficulties in making comparisons over time.

---

[5] This is, of course, a rather artificial calculation since it implies that supply would be available to achieve this.

5

The dynamics of local housing markets

The next three chapters of this report are concerned with the empirical evidence on the dynamics generating the observed patterns of segregation. The two key elements are the operation of local housing markets and the factors that affect the migration and moving decisions of households[1]. Segregation is the outcome of the interaction between these processes and the different elements are brought together in a simulation model. This chapter concentrates on the dynamics of local housing markets. These are important because conventional models typically suggest that if an area experiences low demand, prices will fall, inducing population inflows to those areas. In other words, the market will solve the problem. An alternative view is that low-demand areas experience cumulative circles of decline. Lower prices do not generate inflows of households, rather the expectation of further capital losses lead to further outflows, particularly from higher income households, who are more able to leave. This reinforces segregation. Therefore, understanding how local housing markets, and particularly house prices, work is important to understanding segregation.

A second reason for considering house prices rather than low demand per se is that, as Schill et al (2002) point out, neighbourhood revitalisation is not a precise concept. However, positive outcomes are associated with improved schools, lower crime rates and reduced physical decay. However, if these outcomes occur, they will be capitalised into house prices. Hence, the outcomes are directly observable.

Thresholds in local house prices

In Chapter 2 of this report, discussion of non-linearity explained why thresholds are important conceptually; that is, they are capable of explaining why all local areas do not benefit equally from a general economic expansion and why some areas are left behind. They also imply that spatial targeting is necessary and provide a framework to explain why 'one-size-fits-all' policies do not necessarily work. Local areas have to reach thresholds before they take off and are able to attract private capital. However, the public expenditures necessary to promote the most deprived areas to the take-off point may need to be very large. Furthermore, in Chapter 3, it was suggested that there are good reasons to believe that local housing markets are characterised by thresholds. If so, segregation is more likely to occur. In Britain, there is a large volume of literature on the modelling of house prices at the national and regional level (see Meen, 2001, for a survey), which highlights the main factors influencing price movements. All the models find that prices are determined by the interaction of the demand and supply for housing. However, in all cases, the models assume that the relationship between prices and their determinants are linear. However, for the reasons discussed in Chapter 3, the relationship may be non-linear, exhibiting thresholds in *local* markets. However, currently there are no published results in the UK literature that test this. In this chapter, local

---

[1] This is not to underplay the importance of the labour market, which enters the picture in Chapter 7 of this report.

authority level house prices are explained by the level of deprivation (captured by the 2000 Index of Multiple Deprivation [IMD][2]), incomes and the availability of housing, relative to the number of households. Although this specification is rather simpler than in national price models, it captures the main influences. Our interest is particularly in the relationship between prices and deprivation. As noted earlier in this chapter, any improvements in deprivation, through neighbourhood revitalisation, will be capitalised into prices.

Figure 5.1 graphs the estimated relationship between prices and deprivation (further details are given in Appendix 1 of this report). In order to abstract from region-wide influences, on the horizontal axis, the regional average level of deprivation is subtracted from the level of deprivation in each local authority. Similarly, house prices on the vertical axis are expressed as the local authority median house price relative to the regional maximum. This means that the scale runs between zero and one.

The key result is that the relationship appears, indeed, to be non-linear[3] with threshold values for the Deprivation Index at approximately ± 30 (based on the average of ward scores). Although not shown in Figure 5.1, the curve becomes almost completely flat at values of approximately ± 70. The values are an index, but to give a feel for the magnitudes involved, in the North West the maximum value of the index is 28 in Knowsley (after subtracting the regional average value). Therefore, even the most deprived local authorities are only just around the threshold.

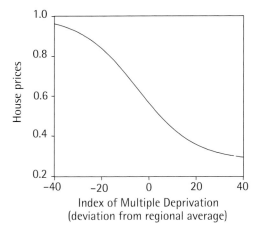

Figure 5.1: Relationship between house prices and deprivation

The main implication of the curve is that policy would have to reduce deprivation (relative to the regional average) in any area to a value of approximately 30, before it will 'take off' of its own accord. If regeneration expenditures only reduce deprivation, say, from 70 to 60, the impact is very modest. Arguably, the trick for both government and private investors is to identify those areas that lie just above the threshold, since modest expenditures generate large returns. Commenting on these findings, Beroube (2005) notes the following:

- The conventional wisdom is that any area can be regenerated given the right level of investment, but this misses the point. Indeed, it might be possible to reduce deprivation from 70 to 30, but the question is whether society has the resources to bring about the desired level of regeneration in all areas. As discussed later in this chapter, the required resources can be very large indeed.
- 'Incremental improvements in social conditions of the most severely deprived communities may produce little market response, and may thus fail to catalyse the broader forces on which regeneration programmes depend. Again these communities are not necessarily beyond "the point of no return", but the effort needed to achieve sustainable improvements in those places, absent some more radical intervention, may exceed what society is willing to expend' (Beroube, 2005, p 35).

---

[2] The index ranks the level of deprivation in every English ward and local authority area. It combines a number of indicators covering income, employment, health deprivation and disability, education, skills and training, housing quality and geographical access to services into a single score for each area.

[3] Testing for thresholds on local authority data is not straightforward, because deprivation for most local authorities lies in the central part of the distribution rather than the tails where the non-linearity should be most evident. Therefore, Meen (2004) devotes a great deal of attention to different tests.

Figure 5.2: Estimated deprivation in the South East, Yorkshire & Humberside, North West and the North East

(i) South East

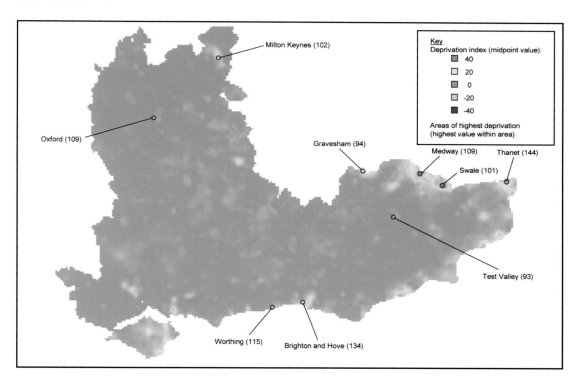

(ii) Yorkshire & Humberside

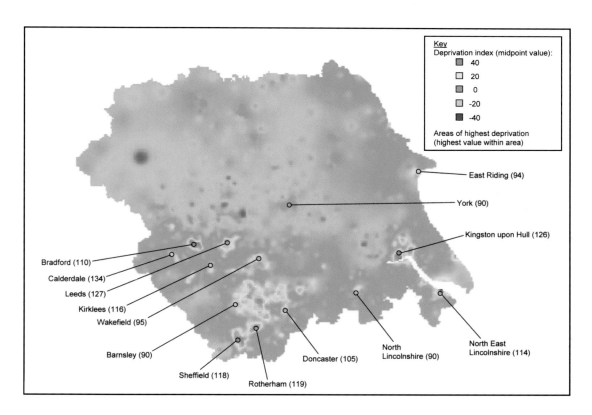

(iii) North West

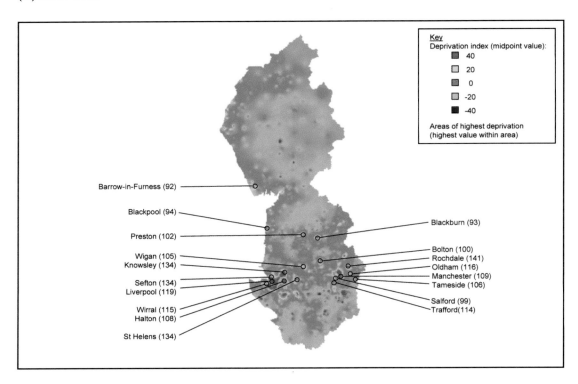

(iv) North East

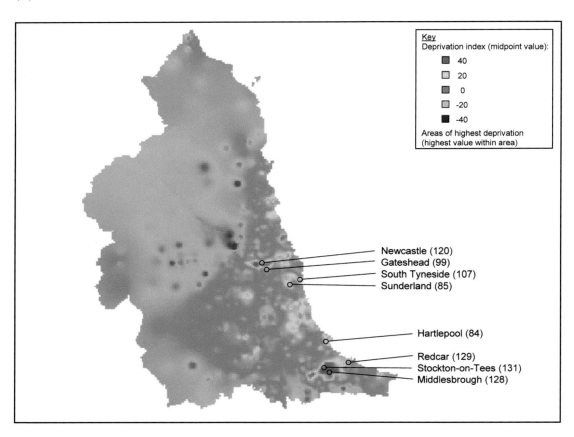

The distribution of deprivation beyond the threshold

Which areas lie beyond the threshold level of deprivation? As we noted earlier in this chapter, no local authority as a whole lies well above the threshold. Most observations lie in the steepest part of the curve. The implication is that no local authority can be 'written off' as a whole; even the most deprived local authorities have their wealthy parts. Consequently, there is no policy ineffectiveness result at the local authority level. This is hardly surprising since most local authorities have a mixture of 'good' and 'bad' areas. This suggests the need to look at deprivation at a finer spatial level. In terms of the 2000 IMD, the next finest spatial scale in England is the ward level. Although details are not presented here, there are few wards that have deprivation values (relative to the regional average) significantly greater than 50. Therefore, in most cases, the most deprived wards are beyond the threshold, but not dramatically so (exceptions are considered later in this chapter).

The 2004 Index (which is highly correlated with the results of the 2000 Index) gives results at the finer Super Output Area (SOA) level. Beroube (2005) gives the number and proportion of SOAs that lie above a level of 40[4]. He defines these as 'extremely deprived SOAs', and the results are reproduced as Table 5.1. Nationally, approximately 1.5% of SOAs fall into this category. However, there is a wide dispersion with a heavy concentration on the North West. It should be remembered that this does not just represent a generally higher level of deprivation in the North West since each is expressed in terms of differences from regional averages.

Further evidence can be obtained at the Output Area (OA) level – the finest spatial disaggregation in the Census. Although the IMD was not constructed at this scale for either the 2000 or 2004 Index, an approximation can be constructed, which is also useful for later analysis. The details of the procedure are given in Meen (2004), but essentially the procedure involves finding a limited number of key variables that explain the main features of the index and which are also published at the OA level in the Census. These variables are, then, weighted together. The weights are obtained from the equations in Table 4.1a in Appendix 4.

Dealing with OAs involves large amounts of data. Therefore, we concentrate on four of the English regions:

- North East (8,599 observations)
- North West (22,710)
- Yorkshire and Humberside (16,793)
- South East (26,646)

Table 5.1: Extremely deprived SOAs (2004)

Region	Extremely deprived SOAs (number)	Extremely deprived SOAs (%)
East Midlands	55	2.0
East	17	0.5
London	14	0.3
North East	31	1.9
North West	190	4.3
South East	26	0.5
South West	31	1.0
West Midlands	53	1.5
Yorks & Humber	77	2.3
England	494	1.5

Source: Beroube (2005)

These are chosen as the areas of highest deprivation, to be contrasted with the region of lowest deprivation. Table 5.1 gives a similar categorisation. The estimated distribution of deprivation at OA level is mapped in Figure 5.2 highlighting the main areas of poverty.

---

[4] Care is needed in applying values from the 2004 Index to equations estimated using the 2000 Index, despite their high correlation, since the methods of construction of the indices is not the same. However, the general conclusions are probably still reasonable.

In each area, three summary measures are presented;

- the proportion of OAs with estimated deprivation indices lying in the range ±30; that is, those lying in the steepest part of the price curve;
- the proportion with values greater than 70, that is, the flattest part of the curve; and
- the standard deviation of scores. Here the interest is in whether the dispersion of outcomes is narrower in the wealthier South East than in the North. Results are given in Table 5.2.

Clearly, the vast majority of OAs lie within the steepest part of the price curve. This is true in all regions and particularly in the South East. It is important to remember, the higher value for the South East does not represent the generally lower level of deprivation in the South, since all calculations are relative to regional means. Most OAs, therefore, are amenable to policy action. However, there are important tails – and these are precisely the areas most typically targeted for action. In the North, slightly more than 1% of OAs have calculated deprivation scores of 70+, but the percentage is much lower in the South East. Although not shown in the table, the tails are concentrated in the older industrial conurbations. In the South East, Kent figures strongly at the top end, particularly OAs within Thanet. Finally, from the standard deviations, it is clear that the distribution is narrower in the South.

As shown in Appendix 4 of this report, quantitatively the unemployment rate is the most important determinant of deprivation, but this possibly presents a statistical problem at fine spatial scales of which we should be aware. There is a negative correlation between population size and the level of deprivation. This means that care has to be taken in interpreting the results at the top end of the distribution. To illustrate, in the North East, Stockton possesses two of the most deprived OAs. The largest value of the Deprivation Index is 131. However, the population of working age is only 117 (the average OA size in the North East is 213), of whom 33 are unemployed, giving an unemployment rate of 28.2%. However, if only three of those found jobs, the index would fall by 11 points. Although the index would, of course, still remain very high, the sensitivity to small numbers is clear. Consequently, the results should be considered in conjunction with the findings at the larger SOA level.

The Five-Year Plan for neighbourhood revitalisation is to target three estates – Harpurhey in Manchester, Gipton in Leeds and Canning Town in Newham[5]. However, we can show how difficult the process of regeneration will prove. Concentrating on Harpurhey, Table 5.3 sets out the characteristics of the ward at the time of the 2001 Census.

Table 5.2: Summary indicators of deprivation in the Census Output Areas

Region	Number of OAs	OAs lying between ±30 (%)	OAs lying above 70 (%)	Standard deviation
North East	8,599	73.5	1.3	27.28
North West	22,710	77.5	1.2	26.18
Yorks & Humber	16,792	78.9	1.2	25.62
South East	26,646	91.6	0.4	18.18

---

[5] The 2005 Budget indicated that six more would be announced.

Table 5.3: Summary indicators for Harpurhey (2001)

	Harpurhey Ward	Manchester	England and Wales
% in employment	41.4	46.4	60.6
% unemployed	6.4	5.0	3.4
% limiting long-term illness	29.8	21.5	18.2
% with no qualifications	51.5	34.0	29.1
% with a degree	8.6	21.4	19.8
% in owner-occupation	33.6	41.8	68.9
% in social housing	52.4	39.4	19.2

Source: Census (2001)

Compared with both Manchester as a whole and England and Wales, Harpurhey has a very low percentage in employment, unemployment almost twice the national average and a poorly educated labour force, predominantly living in social housing. Our work provides an indication of how far some of these variables would have to change in order to bring about a significant reduction in deprivation.

Table 4.1a in Appendix 4 of this report estimates the main factors that contribute to deprivation. The table indicates that, in all regions, unemployment is highly important. The incidence of long-term illness is also a key factor. Ethnicity appears to be more important in the North of the country than the South in explaining deprivation[6]. The table implies that a reduction of one percentage point in the unemployment rate would reduce the IMD by approximately 4.3 points. Therefore, in Harpurhey, for example, if unemployment fell to the Manchester average, deprivation would fall by approximately six points, keeping the other variables constant. Reducing those with long-term illness to the Manchester average might cut deprivation by approximately 16 points. A similar reduction in those with no qualifications is estimated to reduce deprivation by five points. In practice, these factors are all interrelated and a package would affect all. A programme that managed to reduce all three elements to the Manchester average might cut deprivation, therefore, by 27 points. However, since the value of the IMD in Harpurhey in 2000 was 78.28 (48 in terms of the deviation from the regional average), the resource requirements needed to reduce the index to the take-off point of around 30 are likely to be very large.

The dynamics of house prices

All the house price analysis so far is static; that is, it looks at the relationship between prices and deprivation at one point in time, 2001, across the local authorities. However, to explain segregation, the dynamics of change also need to be taken into account. The static relationship might be considered as one measure of the 'fundamentals' towards which the market is adjusting. The deviation of prices from the fundamentals could be considered as a measure of the extent of under- or overvaluation to be corrected in subsequent time periods.

However, given that we only have a measure of disequilibrium in one time period, standard dynamic analysis is not possible and indirect evidence has to be used on the extent to which prices adjust in a manner that clears the market. The first test considers individual local authorities and asks whether there is evidence of significant under- or overvaluation of prices in 2001. Local authorities were identified in the South (East, South East and South West) and North (North East, North West, Yorkshire and Humberside) where the prediction error of the price equation in Appendix 1 of this report was particularly high (formally, where the errors were greater than two standard errors). The percentage changes in prices between 2001 Quarter Three and 2004 Quarter Three in those

---

[6] Bailey and Pickering (2004) find similar results in Scotland.

Table 5.4: Local authority house price change

LAD	Under- or overvalued in 2001	% price change 2001Q3–2004Q3	Regional average % price change 2001Q3–2004Q3
South			
Huntingdonshire	Under	75.8	61.5
Hertsmere	Over	42.0	61.5
Three Rivers	Over	47.3	61.5
Aylesbury Vale	Under	50.0	48.1
Chiltern	Over	42.6	48.1
Dartford	Over	55.1	48.1
Bournemouth	Over	63.6	68.6
Poole	Over	58.3	68.6
Christchurch	Over	50.0	68.6
East Dorset	Over	57.5	68.6
North			
Teesdale	Under	104.2	77.8
Castle Morpeth	Over	70.6	77.8
Hambleton	Over	88.2	94.0
Harrogate	Over	72.7	94.0

authorities were calculated and compared with the relevant regional average growth rates. Over-valued districts in 2001 are expected to show slower than average growth in the subsequent time period. Results are shown in Table 5.4. Except in one case (Dartford), subsequent price changes at least partially eliminated the price disequilibrium.

Although analysis of this form might be used as a basis for predicting price change (and certainly goes beyond an analysis of price to income ratios used by many commentators), this is not its primary purpose. Instead, it shows that there is some evidence that price movements are equilibrating over time. There is no evidence that price behaviour, in itself, adds to segregation of the population. Prices appear to be determined by fundamentals and changes are generally equilibrating. To explain patterns of segregation we need to examine migration movements in conjunction with the housing market. This is the subject of the next two chapters.

Finally, Appendix 1 of this report presents additional evidence on the dynamics of price change and, incidentally, sheds light on the well-known 'ripple effect', where, during a boom, house prices have typically risen first in the South of England with the North gradually catching up over time. The results indicate that prices do adjust to eliminate any disequilibrium – prices clear the market – but adjustment is noticeably quicker in the South.

Conclusions

- Local housing markets (and in particular house prices) behave in the manner that economic theory predicts. Prices respond to differences between demand and supply, although adjustment certainly does not take place immediately, but is spread over a number of years. Therefore, disequilibrium (excess demand or supply) can exist for considerable periods of time.
- Nevertheless, on the evidence available, local housing markets exhibit thresholds that have important consequences for patterns of segregation and the operation of policy. They imply that common (national or regional) shocks have different effects between local areas. Areas with very high levels of deprivation do not benefit equally from positive changes since they need to reach the threshold. This contributes to segregation.
- The areas of high levels of deprivation beyond the thresholds are very localised (although nonetheless important). No local authority as a whole lies above the threshold.
- Thresholds imply the need for spatial targeting of policies. 'One-size-fits-all' policies are not appropriate.
- Thresholds imply that large regeneration expenditures have a different effect from a series of smaller expenditures, which sum to the same total.

6

Migration and location

Patterns of segregation and integration arise from the location decisions of millions of individual households. Governments may provide incentives for households to live in certain areas, but, in the end, households have free choice subject to the constraints of their budgets. In addition to the cost of dwellings and incomes, the choice is typically influenced by demographic characteristics. Young, single-person households, for example, will make different decisions from older households with children. However, all types of households are probably influenced by neighbourhood characteristics.

There are several ways in which these decisions can be analysed. The chapter begins with a description of the characteristics of a sample of movers between 1996 and 2001 for a set of Travel to Work Areas (TTWAs) located in the North and Midlands; data are taken from the British Household Panel Survey (BHPS). The data show that the often-quoted characterisation of movers from the North to the South (notably London) is an oversimplification. In fact, most moves are short distance, within TTWAs and local authorities and even moves that are 'external' are primarily to contiguous locations. This is one indication of the importance of neighbourhood ties – movers are unwilling to disrupt ties to family and friends. The descriptive analysis is supplemented by data taken from the 2002 London Household Survey on moving patterns.

The results from two pieces of empirical analysis are then presented. The first uses Census migration data concentrating on local authority and ward level information. A range of influences on gross flows is identified, but, for our purposes, the key relationship is again with deprivation. In many areas the relationship is non-linear, although the nature of the non-linearities differs from place to place. The results can be used to demonstrate how segregation occurs. The second set of results employs household data from the BHPS and attempts to identify the key factors that influence location choices. Are cultural and sporting facilities critical (as the literature on consumer cities might suggest) or is the traditional concern with school quality and crime paramount?

The characteristics of movers

On the basis of unemployment (Figure 4.1), the most segregated areas lie in the North and Midlands. Therefore, the first part of the analysis concentrates on a sample of TTWAs in these areas. The TTWAs are Bristol, Birmingham, Dudley and Sandwell, Wolverhampton and Walsall, Stoke, Derby, Coventry, Nottingham, Sheffield and Rotherham, Manchester, Leicester, Hull, Middlesbrough and Stockton, Leeds, Bradford, Liverpool, Sunderland and Durham, and Tyneside. The basic criterion for defining a TTWA is that, of the economically active, at least 75% work and live in the area. Household level data for the 18 TTWAs are combined from the BHPS, covering the period 1996-2001. This provides a sample size of 5,691 household year observations. Table 6.1 shows that 8.3% of the sample moved house each year[1], and that 76.2% of moves occurred within local authority boundaries. Moves to a different TTWA account for only 16.2% of all moves.

---

[1] Here, and throughout the analysis, 'movers' refers only to wholly moving households and exclude part-movers.

Table 6.1: Number of moves

	All moves	Moves to a different TTWA	Moves to a different LAD within the same TTWA	Moves within the same LAD
Number of movers	470	76	36	358
Per cent of households	8.3%	1.3%	0.6%	6.3%
Per cent of movers	100%	16.2%	7.7%	76.2%

Table 6.2 shows the proportion of households in each tenure and moving rates according to tenure. The majority of the sample (62.4%) live in owner-occupation, 8.2% of households are private renters and 29.4% live in social housing. Therefore, the share in social housing is rather larger than the national average, but is unsurprising given the choice of sample. Private renters are by far the most mobile group, with 35% of households moving each year. They are also the most likely to migrate to a different TTWA, with 7% doing so each year. Overall mobility rates are lowest for owner-occupiers, with less than 5% moving each year. This largely reflects the higher moving costs associated with this tenure. Households living in social housing have much higher mobility within the same local authority when compared to owner-occupiers: 7.2% of social renters move within the same local authority each year, compared to only 3.4% of owner-occupiers. This represents the well-known churning within the local authority housing stock. However, households living in social housing have very low propensities to move outside their local authority. Only 0.9% of social renters move to a different local authority each year compared to 1.4% of owner-occupiers. Waiting lists hinder households moving to a different local authority. Furthermore, households living in social housing tend to have smaller job search areas and so will be less likely to move to a different TTWA. The percentage of households living in social housing who moved to a different local authority within the same TTWA was 0.5%, greater than the 0.4% of owner-occupiers. However, owner-occupiers were twice as likely to move to a different TTWA compared to social renters.

Table 6.3 shows how the head of household's qualifications affect the propensity to move. Mobility rates are much higher for individuals whose highest qualification is a degree or an A-Level compared to individuals with no qualifications. Individuals with better qualifications are more likely to be employed and will tend to receive higher incomes, enabling them to move more frequently. Furthermore, highly educated individuals tend to have wider job search areas compared to individuals with no or few educational qualifications. As a consequence, individuals with higher qualifications are more likely to move to a different TTWA. Individuals whose highest qualification is an O-Level or GCSE are nearly 40% more likely to move compared to an individual with no qualifications. Individuals with a degree are twice as likely to move when compared to individuals with no qualifications. A potential anomaly is that individuals whose highest qualification is an A-Level are nearly twice as likely to move compared to an individual with a degree. These differences are even more pronounced when moves across TTWAs are examined. Individuals whose highest

Table 6.2: Moves by tenure

	Owner-occupied		Private renter		Social renter	
	Number	%	Number	%	Number	%
Households	3,549	62.4	469	8.2	1,673	29.4
Moved	171	4.8	164	35.0	135	8.1
Moved TTWA	36	1.0	33	7.0	7	0.4
Moved LAD	49	1.4	48	10.2	15	0.9
Moved LAD within TWWA	13	0.4	15	3.2	8	0.5
Moved within LAD	122	3.4	116	24.7	120	7.2

Table 6.3: Moves by household head's qualifications

	Degree		A-Levels		O-Levels and GCSE		No qualifications	
	Number	%	Number	%	Number	%	Number	%
Households	1,835	32.6	542	9.6	1,400	24.9	1,852	32.9
Moved	178	9.7	97	17.9	95	6.8	91	4.9
Moved TTWA	40	2.2	23	4.2	8	0.6	5	0.3

Table 6.4: Moves by household head's age

	Aged 17–21		Aged 22–30		Aged 31–35		Aged 36–40		Aged 41+	
	No	%	No	%	No	%	No	%	No	%
Households	98	1.7	615	10.8	633	11.1	654	11.5	3691	64.9
Moved	56	57.1	132	21.5	64	10.1	46	7.0	172	4.7
Moved TTWA	6	6.1	23	3.7	16	2.5	9	1.4	22	0.6

qualification is an O-Level or GCSE are twice as likely to move to a different TTWA compared to an individual with no qualifications. Individuals with a degree are over seven times as likely to move to a different TTWA when compared to individuals with no qualifications. Furthermore, an individual whose highest qualification is an A-Level is 14 times more likely to move to a different TTWA, compared to an individual with no qualifications.

Table 6.4 shows the relationship between age and the propensity to move. A household's mobility clearly declines with age. This illustrates one of the problems of attracting households back to cities once they have left. Even if neighbourhood conditions are improved in cities, attracting the over-40s back to cities is difficult. Furthermore, as the head of household gets older a household's propensity to migrate to a different TTWA declines. The age bands in Table 6.4 represent life-stage changes. Individuals aged 17-21 have very high mobility rates, with 57.1% moving and 6.1% moving to a different TTWA. This age group is highly mobile, as the persons involved are leaving the parental home, moving to university or taking up employment. Individuals aged 22-30 tend to have high job turnover rates and their moving rates reflect this, with 21.5% moving and 3.7% moving to a different TTWA. Individuals tend to settle down and start families during their 30s, and their moving rates decline as a result. The 40+ age group has the lowest propensity to move with only 4.7% per year doing so. They also have the lowest probability of moving to a different TTWA, with only 0.6% doing so each year.

Table 6.5 shows how the age of children affects the household's propensity to move. The most mobile households are those with a child aged between 0-4; 10.1% of this group moved each year and 1.9% moved to a different TTWA. This may be because households want to move to areas with good schools before children start their education. Once children have started attending a school, parents will be reluctant to move great distances, as they will not want to disrupt their children's education. This is reflected in the low percentage of households with children either aged 5-15 or 16-18 who move to a different TTWA each year (0.8% and 0.7% respectively). Notice for later use, however, that *in absolute terms*, the largest numbers of movers are those without any children, reflecting their weighting in the sample. This influences the factors that are found to be important in determining location.

In summary, the tables indicate that:

- most movers are young, without children and are educated; and
- most moves are within the same local authority and/or TTWA.

Table 6.5: Moves by age of children

	No children aged 0-18		Has a child aged 0-4		Has a child aged 5-15		Has a child aged 16-18	
	Number	%	Number	%	Number	%	Number	%
Households	3,942	69.3	634	11.1	1,326	23.3	141	2.5
Moved	322	8.2	64	10.1	109	8.2	11	7.8
Moved TTWA	58	1.5	12	1.9	10	0.8	1	0.7

Table 6.6: Migrants to London from other regions: most-favoured boroughs (% of total migrants of a given age into London)

All ages (*n*=580)	Age 25-29 (*n*=132)
Kingston (6.9%)	Haringey (9.8%)
Haringey (4.7%)	Enfield (6.1%)
Hounslow (4.7%)	Camden (5.3%)
Hammersmith (4.3%)	Newham (5.3%)
Hillingdon (4.1%)	Hammersmith (4.5%)
Wandsworth (4.1)	Lambeth (4.5%)
Sutton (4.0%)	Wandsworth (4.5%)
Richmond (3.8%)	Croydon (3.8%)
Enfield (3.6%)	Kingston (3.8%)
Redbridge (3.6%)	Redbridge (3.8%)

Source: extracted by Suzanne Dixon from London Household Survey (2002)

Although these findings are certainly not new and hold internationally, they are worth highlighting since they inform the empirical results and the later policy conclusions.

The second set of results comes from the 2002 London Household Survey. The survey has the advantage that current and previous locations are identified at a fine spatial level (postcode). The disadvantage is that, by its nature, the survey only covers in-migration to London. There is no information on movers from London to other regions or internationally.

Table 6.6 looks at the 10 most common destinations, by borough, of inter-regional migrants into London since 1991. The first column looks at all migrants, and the second at the 25-29 age group. The 20-24 group is not considered because of the distortions introduced by a high number of students. Although migrants are, by no means, concentrated on just a few boroughs, some features stand out.

First, the most common destination for migrants of all ages is Kingston. Richmond is also in the top 10 and these are the boroughs with the lowest levels of deprivation and best performance in terms of school examination results[2]. Second, across all ages, Outer London boroughs feature highly, but the pattern differs considerably for the younger age group. Inner London boroughs and those experiencing higher levels of deprivation are more important than for migrants as a whole. Prima facie, it appears that a different set of factors influences the location choices of young migrants, although the deprived boroughs of Hackney and Tower Hamlets are not popular among either age group.

---

[2] Kingston is also likely to gain from its location as a 'peninsula' jutting out into Surrey. Therefore, it is particularly likely to attract migrants from Surrey.

Table 6.7: Area characteristics – Hammersmith

	Hammersmith
Owner-occupation rate	43.95
Gross in-migration	15,830
Gross out-migration	17,813
Net migration	–1,983
Percentage population in full-time employment	53.56%
Percentage population unemployed	4.95%
Percentage population with no qualifications	17.93%
Percentage population with a degree	45.07%

Source: Census 2001

Inner-London Hammersmith is a popular choice for all ages and it is worth comparing the characteristics of the borough with those of Harpurhey, shown in Chapter 5 of this report. Perhaps, the most striking statistic in Table 6.7 is that, whereas Harpurhey has more than half of its residents with no educational qualifications, almost half of Hammersmith residents have a degree. Since we found in Table 6.3, that those with the highest educational qualifications are the most mobile, it is unsurprising that the population of Hammersmith has a turnover rate (the sum of in-migration and out-migration per capita) of 20% per annum. The turnover rate is aided by the high proportion of residents in the private-rented sector and the youth of the population (15% of its population are aged 25-29).

Moving households: information from the Census

The conclusions from the descriptive analysis in the previous section are reinforced by the econometric results. The first set of results attempts to explain the migration flows in the 2001 Census. The information in the Census refers to moves by individuals over the previous year. We have expressed the flows as a percentage of the resident population. The earlier descriptive analysis (and previous work in the literature) suggests that the following variables are likely to be an important part of the explanation:

1. Local levels of deprivation
2. Age structure of the local population
3. Tenure structure
4. Changing labour demand
5. Housing availability and vacancies
6. Housing costs

The combination of variables allows us to test the relative importance of different equilibrating mechanisms. If migration inflows are, for example, strongly negatively related to house prices or positively to vacancies, then adverse shocks to any area may be self-correcting[3]. Alternatively, if the level of deprivation (which captures a range of neighbourhood characteristics) is the most important factor, negative shocks may build upon each other. In addition, areas that have high percentages of young individuals are likely to experience higher rates of both inflows and outflows. Moreover, areas that have high proportions of renters are expected to have greater mobility. Areas where unemployment is increasing are unlikely to be attractive to migrants.

---

[3] Although price falls may stabilise migration outflows, the literature recognises that expectations of capital losses may lead to further flows away from the most deprived areas. This is part of the 'cumulative process of decline' observed in low demand areas and also results from the non-linear price relationships discussed in Chapter 5 of this report.

Table 2.1a in Appendix 2 of this report presents the econometric results for gross migration flows at the local authority level, but separate equations are estimated for the local authorities within the North, Midlands, the South and London. The data exclude intra-local authority moves, but it is still the case that most moves are relatively short distance rather than inter-regional.

All these factors are found to be statistically important and are discussed in more detail in Appendix 2 of this report. However, here, we are particularly concerned with the relationship between migration and deprivation. As noted earlier in this report, if the relationship is strong, cumulative outflows and segregation are likely to result. Furthermore, Appendix 2 indicates that the relationship between migration and deprivation is non-linear, although the precise form varies between regions. Figure 6.1 plots the relationship estimated for the London boroughs[4].

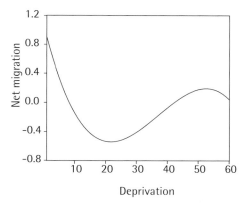

Figure 6.1: The relationship between net migration and deprivation – London

In Figure 6.1, the *net* flows are graphed although these are based on separate relationships for the gross flows (see Appendix 2 of this report). However, although London is often characterised as an area of net population loss through inter-regional migration, the picture is, in fact, slightly more complex. In the areas of very low deprivation (at values of the index lying between 0 and 10), the net inflows are strong and positive, using the average values of the remaining variables in the equations. However, only Kingston and Richmond fall into this category. This matches the results in Table 6.6 (although from a different data source), where Kingston was found to be a particularly attractive location for migrants (although to a lesser extent for young migrants). Figure 6.1 shows that net flows are negative over 'moderate' ranges of deprivation (10-40), but become positive again at high levels of deprivation, although the net flows are weaker. Again this broadly matches the flows of the young in Table 6.6. Figure 6.1 suggests that net inflows are positive at values of the Deprivation Index greater than 40, but begin to decline again at values greater than 55. Haringey, Southwark and Islington fall into the Deprivation Index range 40-55 and Table 6.6 indicates that Haringey has been the most popular location for young migrants (Newham lies just outside the range with a value of 56).

Figure 6.2 plots the estimated relationship between migration and deprivation for Greater Manchester. However, in this case, the equation is estimated across the wards. Therefore, it takes into account intra-local authority moves over ward boundaries. Since the results are used in Chapter 7 of this report, the relationship is plotted for gross inflows and outflows as well as net flows. The position is very different from London: beyond moderate levels of deprivation, net outflows accelerate, contributing to vicious circles of decline. The graphs suggest that it is outflows, rather than inflows, that mostly generate these forces; inflows are approximately linearly related to deprivation, whereas outflows are non-linear – outflows speed up at high deprivation levels (see Table 2.2a in Appendix 2). These flows reinforce patterns of segregation since anyone who can leave will do so. In summary, the migration flows are destabilising and the effect of deprivation is very strong on migration flows.

Moving and location: evidence from the household data

Household data taken from the BHPS allow us to look deeper into the factors affecting location and moving decisions. Implicitly, these factors lie behind the aggregate flows analysed in the

---

4 The graph sets the values for the remaining variables in the equations at their means.

Figure 6.2: The relationship between net migration and deprivation – wards in Greater Manchester

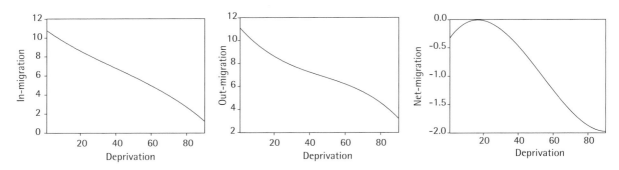

previous section, but the questions examined have policy significance. The analysis begins with a model of the factors that affect moving. The earlier data from the BHPS are again used, covering TTWAs predominantly in the North and Midlands. London is a notable exclusion. An obvious, but often missed, issue is that there is little point in providing high quality facilities to attract certain socioeconomic groups if these groups have a low probability of ever moving. Policies that target the most mobile are more likely to be successful.

Table 3.1a in Appendix 3 of this report presents the results of the model aimed at explaining moving decisions. Here, in each year, households have to make a decision either to move home or stay where they are. The decision will depend on the socioeconomic characteristics of the household. The equation includes the key household characteristics at the beginning of this chapter, notably: age, employment status, income, marital status change, and tenure. Appendix 3 shows that all these variables are statistically significant, with the exception of the *level* of household income, which is strongly correlated with employment status. However, the *change* in income is significant. Arguably, we should expect this to be more important than the level of income. The results also show how moving propensities decline with age. From the marginal effects (not shown in the table), a household with a head aged 22-30 is four times more likely to move than a household with a head aged 40+.

The values in Table 3.1a have to be interpreted relative to a reference group. In the case of employment status, the reference group is the unemployed. Table 3.1a indicates that all the groups of employed and self-employed have higher moving probabilities than the unemployed, since the signs are positive. Furthermore, those on the highest incomes have the highest moving propensities.

For tenure, private renters are the control group and Table 3.1a indicates that both owners and social renters have lower moving probabilities, but owners are significantly less mobile than social renters. However, as we see later in this report, this only holds for moves within the local authority (which are the majority of moves). As noted earlier in this chapter, social renters are churning within a (poor quality) local authority housing stock. It does not mean that social tenants are fundamentally more mobile. Finally, students, those changing jobs or experiencing marital status change are all mobile.

In summary, we can already begin to see some of the factors that lead to segregation. Older households, those on low incomes, the unemployed and those in social housing are all likely to suffer from low mobility (and from what follows, are less likely to break out of the worst locations). By contrast the wealthy, the young and the high skilled have higher moving propensities and are in a better position to move to the most attractive neighbourhoods. It is no coincidence that regenerated cities worldwide have relied heavily on this socioeconomic group

The next issue is to identify the factors, which can be influenced by policy, that are likely to attract (high-income) movers. However, note that from Tables 6.4 and 6.5, most movers are young and have no children. Therefore, the factors that are likely to be found significant will be those that are important to this group. The results are divided into two sets. The first set examines the influences on choice between different TTWAs, whereas the second looks at the choice of local authority within TTWAs. Ideally, we would also have liked to examine choices within local authorities, but the disaggregation available in the BHPS and the sample sizes did not make this feasible. However, in general, we expect the longer-distance moves across TTWAs to be more influenced by labour market factors, whereas shorter-distance moves within the TTWA are likely to be affected chiefly by housing and neighbourhood variables. Moves within the TTWA dominate the data set.

Table 3.2a in Appendix 3 of this report considers the key factors influencing the choice between TTWAs, which are a combination of individual characteristics and location variables[5]. The table indicates that students, the low skilled, those aged 40+ and social renters are all less likely to move outside the current TTWA. The low skilled typically have smaller job search areas. Again the low skilled are more likely to become trapped within their current location.

The table also shows that those moving for job related reasons are more likely to leave the TTWA, but area characteristics influence the choice of location. In line with earlier work by Meen (2001) for London and the South East, and the Census results from earlier in this chapter, high levels of deprivation provide unattractive locations for migrants. Areas with high levels of unemployment are also unattractive, although the coefficents are insignificant. This probably arises from the high correlation between deprivation and unemployment (see Table 4.1a).

Again, these results point to increasing segregation over time. Even if they are able to move, the lowest skilled are less likely to move outside the TTWA and, from the next section, are more likely to be in the worst areas.

Table 3.3a considers the choice between different local authorities within the TTWA. At this level, more emphasis is placed on the neighbourhood characteristics rather than individual attributes. Although age, job-related moves and marital change are included in Table 3.3a, they are barely significant. In addition, the number of children in the age band 5-15, which is expected to reduce moving across local authorities, has only a limited effect. However, the equation includes a number of quality indicators over which the local authority has some influence, notably:

- satisfaction with cultural facilities;
- satisfaction with sporting facilities;
- council tax payments;
- percentage of school pupils obtaining 5+ GCSEs, grades A-C; and
- standard deviation of GCSE results across schools in the local authority.

These sets of variables, which are related to those chosen by Egan (2004) to measure sustainability, capture a combination of influences, potentially appealing to young high-income households; that is, the main movers. Particular attention is paid to elements of 'consumer cities'.

Table 3.3a indicates that the quality of sporting and cultural factors has a significant positive effect on the choice of location[6]. However, the level of council tax payments has a negative impact. Since the quality of local services and their cost, presumably, is positively related, we expect the two factors to be at least partly offsetting in their impact on location choice, although large-scale regeneration is, of course, not generally funded out of council tax revenues. It should be noted, however, that the catchment areas for cultural facilities are wider than just the local authority. The improved

---

[5] Nested multinomial logit models have also been estimated in which location and moving decisions are modelled together. The results are not presented here although they are generally in line with the simpler logit specifications.

[6] Satisfaction with park facilities and cleanliness of the local authority were also tested. Although these were found to have some impact, they are correlated with the other satisfaction indicators and, consequently, the significance of these other variables falls.

facilities of Hulme, for example (a case study in Chapter 8 of this report) are used by individuals living outside the area. Similarly, the Lowry Centre is in Salford, but is a major cultural asset to all Mancunians. The point is that households do not necessarily have to live in an area to experience the benefits – the advantages spill over to others. Nevertheless, there is empirical evidence to suggest that these facilities do improve the attractiveness of an area for living as well as visiting.

Disentangling the influence of school quality is difficult. First, there are problems of measurement. Indicators based on GCSE scores tell us as much about the economic status of the local residents as about the quality of the school. Alternatively, scores are an outcome of the location process rather than a cause. If high-skilled, high-income residents are attracted to an area, in time, the quality of the schools, measured in GCSE scores, will improve. Second, as already noted, most movers in the sample do not have children and, therefore, are likely to attach a lower priority to schools than existing residents. This does not mean that the traditional concern with schools is misplaced. Indeed, we argue in a subsequent chapter that good-quality schools are crucial to retaining households at a later stage in their life cycles, but they are not necessarily critical in attracting young households in the first place.

In fact, high levels and rates of change of unemployment are found to act as a deterrent to movers and, if unemployment is included in the equation, the GCSE variable has a perverse effect, that is, households appear to be attracted to the areas with the worst schools, although they will avoid areas of highest unemployment. The education findings are not plausible and, overall, our conclusion is that it is difficult to disentangle the influence of education on location choice. Simply looking at the coefficients can be misleading.

Finally, it should be noticed that the equation includes no house price variables. The reason is that much of the price variation between local authorities within the TTWA will reflect the difference in local services, neighbourhood conditions and council tax payments already included in the model. Within the TTWA there should be little true variation in quality-adjusted prices.

Conclusions

- The factors that affect mobility and migration flows are consistent on both aggregate Census and household data. Aggregate migration flows to and from any area are influenced by levels of deprivation, the age structure of the population, the tenure distribution, labour market conditions and the availability of housing. Young, high-income, highly qualified individuals without children are the most mobile.
- However, most moves are short distance. Trying to induce long-distance moves (for example, from the South to the North) is very difficult.
- Similarly, since the propensity to move falls sharply with age, attempts to attract middle-aged people to any location to improve social mix is difficult.
- Since most movers are young, there is evidence that their choice of location is affected by the quality of sporting and cultural facilities. However, young, high-income groups try to avoid areas of high unemployment and high council tax bills.
- The relationship between migration and deprivation is strong and non-linear and this reinforces segregation patterns.
- The role of school quality on location choice cannot be adequately assessed from our sample.

7

Explaining patterns of deprivation and segregation

The previous two chapters have considered, in detail, two of the key factors determining segregation patterns: the operation of local housing markets and the determinants of migration. However, to explain the constancy of segregation over the past 20 years and to consider prospects for the future, they need to be brought together into a full simulation model. In this chapter, the results of a simulation model for the English local authorities and the wards of the North West Government Office Region are discussed. This is the first model of its type in Britain; although we have stressed that deprivation and segregation are not the same concept, the relationship between them can be explored in the model.

A model of the English local authorities

We begin with an econometric model of the 354 English local authorities. The model covers, house prices, migration (using the results of the earlier chapters), incomes, deprivation and labour market status.

Table 4.1a in Appendix 4 of this report provides details of the key factors affecting deprivation, where deprivation is measured by the 2000 Index of Multiple Deprivation (IMD)[1]. One of the most noticeable features is that the index can be explained by a limited range of factors that are recorded in the Census[2]. The equations are estimated across all the English local authorities and disaggregated by region, but typically the same set of variables turns out to be important in all regions.

In all cases, unemployment is a major influence. It is most unlikely that deprivation can be reduced in the worst areas without a major reduction in unemployment. This can occur either through improving the employment prospects of existing residents or through the arrival of high-skilled migrants. The incidence of long-term illness is also a key factor. An absence of qualifications has a more variable effect, but this is because of the high correlation between qualifications and unemployment. Ethnicity appears to be more important in the North of the country than the south in explaining deprivation. However, as the final row of Table 4.1a shows, black individuals are noticeably more likely to suffer deprivation than Asians.

Perhaps, contrary to expectations, the model does not include any relationship between deprivation and tenure. It is undoubtedly true that areas of high deprivation are associated with heavy concentrations of social housing, but this does not necessarily imply that social housing *causes* deprivation. The appropriate causality tests are, however, difficult to conduct on cross-section data. However, our model does imply that low levels of owner-occupation and high deprivation typically go together.

---

[1] The 2004 Index produces very similar results since the two indices are highly correlated.

[2] Bailey and Pickering (2004) reach similar conclusions for Scotland.

Table 4.2a in Appendix 4 of this report examines the factors that affect labour market status. Growth and labour demand in any local area are influenced by a combination of national, regional and local factors. Declining national and regional economies will clearly affect local economies to a greater or lesser extent. However, our interest concerns differences in performance by local authorities within each region. Therefore, as noted earlier in this report, the model adjusts for regional conditions across the country by taking the differences from regional averages for each local area. This means that the emphasis is on supply-side influences. In other words, the model abstracts from differing conditions that arise from region-wide demand levels. In particular, the proportions of individuals in full-time employment, part-time employment and unemployment depend primarily on the proportion of individuals with particular levels of skills in each area. Areas with high numbers of skilled individuals are less likely to decline. This is one reason why the North to South drift of the most highly skilled is of particular importance.

For the model, the working population is divided into the proportions in full-time employment, part-time employment and unemployed. (The proportions do not add up to one, but they are sufficient for our purposes.) The variables determining labour market status are:

- the proportion of the local authority's population with no qualifications and Level One qualifications (these are the basic school leaving qualifications usually taken at age 16);
- the proportion of young individuals in the population;
- the presence of long-term illness;
- gender; and
- the percentage of black individuals.

In the results, the importance of an absence of qualifications stands out. The proportion employed full time is clearly lower and the proportion unemployed is far higher. Since, from Chapter 5 of this report, Harpurhey has 51% of its residents without qualifications, it is unsurprising that unemployment is twice the national average. Even basic qualifications (Level One) raise the probability of employment. The proportion in part-time employment is higher among females. Long-term illness raises unemployment and reduces employment. Unemployment is positively related to the proportion of black individuals in the local authority. Those in the 16-24 age group are less likely to be employed, since they have a higher probability of being at school or in higher education. Individuals in the 25-29 age group are more likely to be employed full time or to be unemployed than to be in part-time employment.

The final relationship required to complete the model determines local income (apart from identities or adding-up conditions). The details are shown as Equation 3 in Appendix 4. Local authority average income is strongly positively related to the proportion of the local population in full-time employment, but declines with part-time employment and unemployment. A graduate premium also exists in that local average incomes are strongly related to the proportion holding degree-level qualifications or the equivalent.

The equations in the appendices can be used to construct models for any or all of the English local authorities. As a sample, four local authorities are chosen: two from the North (Knowsley in the North West and Kingston-upon-Hull in Yorkshire and Humberside), and two in the South (Reading in the South East and Southend-on-Sea in the East). The two northern districts are among the most deprived in the country, whereas Reading lies along the expanding M4 corridor. Southend is a seaside town on the east coast and lies at the edge of the Thames Gateway, which has been targeted for an expansion in house building over the next 10 years.

Key indicators are given in Table 7.1. Clearly, although the areas have similarly sized populations (except Hull), each of the local authority districts exhibits different characteristics. The level of deprivation in Knowsley is almost three times as high as in Reading. House prices in Reading in 2001 averaged £123,500 compared with £37,500 in Hull. However, in terms of affordability (measured as the ratio of median house prices to average household incomes), Reading is the worst placed. Affordability in Hull was only 1.5 times incomes. Similarly, most households could probably afford to move to Knowsley from other parts of the country.

The income discrepancies reflect both the relative proportions in full-time work and the level of qualifications. In the southern districts, full-time employment is approximately 50% of the population, but only 37% in Knowsley and 39% in Hull. The proportion with degree level qualifications in Reading is approximately three times that in Knowsley and Hull.

Table 7.1 also shows that Reading has a noticeably higher proportion of individuals in the mobile 25-29 age band. This is reflected in the migration rates. Turnover, measured as the sum of migration inflows and outflows as a percentage of the resident population, was 14.2% in the Census year, compared with 5.8% in Knowsley, 6.5% in Kingston and 7.4% in Southend[3]. In line with the results in Chapter 6 of this report, moving outside the local authority boundaries declines with incomes, although turnover *within* the district may remain high. From Table 7.1, household income in Knowsley and Hull is only approximately two thirds of that in Reading.

The models can be used to examine the question of whether districts are likely to converge or diverge in the future in terms of the level of deprivation. This is not quite the same question as to whether segregation will increase or decrease. It is possible for deprivation in a local authority as a whole to increase relative to other districts, but for segregation within the local authority to decline.

Table 7.1: Area characteristics (2001)

	Knowsley	Reading	Southend	Kingston-upon-Hull
Index of Deprivation (2000)	58.22	19.73	23.26	44.70
Affordability	2.23	3.29	2.64	1.52
Median house prices	£54,000	£123,500	£84,000	£37,500
Number of households	60,553	57,877	70,978	104,288
Owner-occupation rate	61.72%	66.67%	72.76%	52.20%
Gross in-migration	4,197	10,088	6,234	7,551
Gross out-migration	4,499	10,203	5,625	8,282
Net migration	−302	−115	609	−731
Total population	150,459	143,096	160,257	243,589
Population share 16-24	11.04%	15.04%	9.54%	12.75%
Population share 25-29	5.83%	10.23%	6.28%	6.89%
% population in full-time employment	37.33%	53.47%	46.95%	39.34%
% population unemployed	5.87%	2.52%	3.65%	6.23%
% population with no qualifications	43.00%	22.83%	29.79%	41.20%
% population with Level 4/5 qualifications	9.86%	28.26%	13.64%	9.94%
Household income	24,201	37,503	31,870	24,650
Headship rate	40.25%	40.44%	44.29%	42.81%

---

[3] Although not shown in the table, turnover is much higher in London than in Reading. The young, high-skilled population in Hammersmith, for example, yields a turnover rate of 20% per annum.

One way of approaching the question is to ask how areas respond to changes over which they have little or no control. Are there self-equilibrating mechanisms within the districts or do the changes worsen the disparities? Of course, there are many changes that could be examined, but given the importance attached by the model to skills and qualifications, we concentrate on this aspect. As in Chapter 6 of this report, the outcomes are dependent on migration flows and the operation of housing markets. One view is that skills improvements worsen local conditions in deprived areas, because those with higher skills and incomes find it easier to leave. Andersson and Bråmå (2004), for example, find supporting survey evidence for this effect in Sweden. This is also consistent with the household results of Chapter 6 . However, this is not the issue examined here. The question is not whether an *individual* with improved skills will leave a deprived area, but, instead, if an *area* manages to raise its skills base, are net migration outflows reduced?

In the model simulation (Table 7.2), the proportion of individuals with no qualifications is reduced by two percentage points in each location[4]. Each is assumed to obtain a Level One qualification. As we have stressed, skills levels are important. The improvement reduces the number unemployed, offset by a rise in the proportion in full-time employment. This, in turn, increases local incomes, reduces deprivation and raises the turnover of the housing stock through migration. However, note that, although turnover rises, the net effect on migration is fairly modest. Hence, despite the strong dynamics, the overall population size remains stable. Therefore, in these four local authorities, educational improvements lead to gains in terms of reducing deprivation. Furthermore, house prices in most cases rise faster than incomes, reflecting lower levels of deprivation. The exception is Knowsley, the district with the highest level of deprivation in Table 7.1. This is consistent with the non-linear results from Chapter 5 of this report. The reduction in deprivation in Knowsley is only 1.5 percentage points and this is insufficient to take the area to the take-off point. Finally, perhaps the central finding is that equal skills improvements across the four districts have a disproportionate effect on the most disadvantaged areas in terms of migration. Although skills improvements raise both inflows and outflows in all districts, the net flows are only positive in the two disadvantaged areas. In this sense, skills improvements encourage a reduction in inequality, although the effects are modest and take time. It is unsurprising that poverty is persistent.

Table 7.2: Effects of an improvement in skills

	Knowsley	Reading	Southend	Kingston–upon–Hull
Index of Deprivation (points)	−1.48	−1.29	−1.19	−1.22
Affordability (points)	−0.02	0.10	0.08	0.02
Median house prices (%)	1.18	4.34	3.63	3.13
Gross in-migration (%)	4.21	2.50	3.46	2.11
Gross out-migration (%)	3.20	2.80	4.00	1.83
Net migration (numbers)	38.80	−27.82	−27.44	20.56
Total population (%)	0.163	−0.093	−0.088	0.151
% population in full-time employment (points)	1.13	1.88	1.23	1.32
% population unemployed (points)	−0.215	−0.184	−0.159	−0.16
% population with no qualifications (points)	−2.10	−1.90	−1.90	−2.00
% population with Level 4/5 qualifications (points)	0.107	−0.036	−0.048	0.093
Household income (%)	1.90	1.67	1.16	1.99

---

[4] The simulation is conducted by solving the model (in Excel) from the starting point in 2001 up to 2011. This gives a baseline scenario. The qualifications variables, then, are changed over the whole time period and the differences from the base calculated. The results shown in Table 7.2 are the differences from the base in the final year, 2011. This year is chosen as it is the next Census year.

A model of the North West wards

The estimates of segregation, using Indices of Dissimilarity in Chapter 4 of this report, were calculated across the wards of the local authorities. Therefore, if we are to examine how segregation is generated, a ward level model is required. In terms of data alone, this is a major undertaking, although the heavy reliance on the Census means that most of the information is readily available. However, to limit the size of the undertaking, this section concentrates on the North West, which in itself covers more than 1,000 wards of which Harpurhey is one. The model covers all the variables in the local authority version and adopts the same basic structure, but the finer spatial scale introduces additional issues. The main difference concerns migration. Whereas the local authority model only needed to consider inter-local authority moves, now intra-district moves are explicitly modelled. This implies that the number of moves expands considerably and the majority are short distance. For example, Table 7.1 indicates there were almost 4,500 out-migrants from Knowsley. The equivalent figure summed over the wards of Knowsley is almost 11,000. The difference between the two represents moves between the Knowsley wards. The relationship between migration and deprivation for the North West wards is again non-linear. As discussed earlier in this chapter, the non-linearity contributes to the dynamics of segregation. With the exception of the migration equations, an important simplifying assumption is made: it is assumed that the structure and coefficients of the house price, employment status, deprivation and income equations are the same as in the local authority versions. In addition to operating as a simplification, this has the advantage of allowing us to consider a model that is consistent at the different spatial scales.

The model allows us to consider any set of wards, but the key issues can be demonstrated by concentrating on Manchester. First, assume that the proportion of residents in all the Manchester wards with no qualifications falls by five percentage points, compensated by a corresponding rise of those with Level One qualifications. The model suggests that the Dissimilarity Index for Manchester as a whole (measured in terms of unemployment, as in Table 4.1) would *rise* by 0.03 points. In other words, a general improvement in skills, which leads to a general reduction in unemployment, increases the segregation of those who remain unemployed and do not benefit from the skills improvement. In order to reduce segregation, measures have to be spatially targeted, but note that the effect on the Dissimilarity Index is modest. In all the simulations that we have conducted, a common feature is that it is difficult to produce large changes to the segregation index. It is, therefore, unsurprising that the studies identified in Chapter 4 of this report find little evidence

Table 7.3: Effects of improvements in skills in Harpurhey

	% no qualifications −2	% no qualifications −20	% no qualifications −30	% no qualifications −40
Gross in-migration (numbers)	24	190	268	351
Gross out-migration (numbers)	22	155	212	268
Net migration (numbers)	3	36	56	82
Turnover (% points)	0.51	3.43	4.53	5.63
Unemployment (numbers)	−18	−129	−180	−236
Unemployment (% points)	−0.34	−2.46	−3.39	−4.40
House prices (%)	2.75	43.70	85.50	151.90
Income (%)	1.41	11.40	16.70	23.50
Affordability (% points)	0.02	0.38	0.76	1.35
Deprivation (points)	−1.96	−15.80	−22.40	−29.30
Population (%)	0.4	4.5	7.1	10.2
Dissimilarity Index (Manchester)	−0.0008	−0.0031	−0.0006	0.0024

of changes in the index over the past 20 years. Similarly, our base scenario used in simulations, constructed over the period 2001-11, suggests little change is likely to occur over the next Census period.

Second, given its special status, Harpurhey provides a good case study[5]. Chapter 5 of this report examined the sensitivity of deprivation in Harpurhey to changes in unemployment and illness in a partial framework. These results can now be embedded into the full model. If the percentage of the Harpurhey population with no qualifications, the percentage with degrees and the proportion suffering long-term illness reach the Manchester average, deprivation would reach the take-off point, but segregation in Manchester as a whole would only fall very modestly since Harpurhey is only one of 34 wards (at the Census date).

Third, if the sensitivity of Harpurhey (and other wards of extreme deprivation) to variations in the proportion with no qualifications is examined, some unexpected results emerge. Table 7.3 considers key variables from the model, expressed in terms of deviations from a base scenario. The respective columns attempt to show what would happen if the percentage of the population with no qualifications was reduced in turn by 2, 20, 30 and 40 points.

The simulations demonstrate the importance of take-off points in the housing market. A reduction in the proportion with no qualifications of two percentage points is estimated to increase house prices by 3%, an improvement of 20 points raises prices by 44% and an improvement in qualifications of 40 points raises prices by approximately 150%. This is a reflection of Figure 5.1. The larger change takes the ward beyond the take-off point. Alternatively, although Table 7.3 shows that both income and deprivation rise proportionately between the scenarios, house prices rise disproportionately. This, in turn, implies affordability (measured as the ratio of median house prices to average household incomes) worsens sharply as deprivation falls beyond the thresholds. This implies that an increasing percentage of skilled residents in the area worsens affordability unless accompanied by an increase in good quality housing supply.

Finally, note that although a reduction of 20 points reduces segregation in Manchester as a whole, a reduction of 40 points *raises* segregation. As Harpurhey heads towards the Manchester average, the concentration of the unemployed in other wards becomes greater, increasing segregation. Therefore, improvements in skills in an area of high deprivation do not uniformly reduce the level of segregation in the local authority as a whole.

Fourth, it was suggested earlier that areas lying close to the threshold require particular attention. Areas just above the deprivation threshold can be improved by relatively modest expenditures, whereas areas just below the threshold could easily tip into decline. In order to demonstrate this and the effects on segregation, an additional Manchester ward, Sharston, is chosen, which lies closer to the threshold than Harpurhey. In Table 7.4, the effect of increasing and decreasing the proportion with no qualifications by 15 points is considered. The table shows that, although the changes are symmetric, the effects on the local economy are not. The case in which the skills base worsens has a disproportionate effect on population and deprivation because of the increased migration outflows. The poorer skills base tips Sharston into decline. From Figure 6.2, Sharston is operating along the steepest part of the migration curve. Since the more highly skilled have a greater propensity to migrate, unemployment and deprivation rise significantly. Furthermore, segregation increases (for the same reasons as in Harpurhey, a reduction in the percentage with no qualifications also increases segregation). Areas close to the threshold potentially face dangers of tipping into spirals of decline.

---

[5] It might be noted that Harpurhey has already committed itself to district centre redevelopment, including a concentration of public service facilities for example, new leisure facilities and a children's centre. These are consistent with the findings of our location models.

In summary, the simulation demonstrates that segregation is a complex phenomenon. Improvements in skills in the most deprived areas of any local authority do not necessarily lead to a reduction in segregation in the local authority as a whole.

Table 7.4: Effects of improvements in skills in Sharston

	% no qualifications −15	% no qualifications +15
Net migration (numbers)	59	−78
Unemployment (% points)	−1.55	4.65
House prices (%)	62	−44
Deprivation (points)	−10.6	23.9
Population (%)	4.4	−6.9
Dissimilarity Index (Manchester)	0.005	0.014

8

Mixed communities: evidence from case studies

The issues

Case studies can be used to shed further light on the dynamics of mixed communities in a different way from formal modelling. The case studies were carried out in three areas across England and are particularly concerned with changes in the tenure distribution over time. In addition to providing evidence arising from interviews with key stakeholders in the communities (see Appendix 5 of this report for details), the chapter links up with the work in the earlier chapters, by comparing perceptions of change with the evidence of actual change between the 1991 and 2001 Censuses. The aim is to consider areas where both social/affordable housing has been inserted in predominantly owner-occupied markets and also attempts to introduce and sustain private housing for sale in social housing areas. We do not try to be representative; rather, we look at examples where, on the face of it, interventions appear to have generated mixed-tenure communities. How has this happened and are the perceptions matched by the reality of tenure change? The three case studies chosen are:

- Werrington in Peterborough
- Newbiggin Hall in Newcastle-upon-Tyne
- Hulme in Manchester

The key research questions addressed in the interviews were:

- How did these communities become mixed?
- What factors explain the case study experience, for example, local contextual drivers; compositional characteristics of residents; neighbourhood effects; specific policy initiatives?
- Are the observed tenure changes sustainable?
- What broader lessons does this stage of the work have for the project as a whole?

The main case study instruments involved secondary data collection, literature review, local government and associated records of, for example, policy initiatives and data on key residential developments. Key actor interviews were carried out with local government housing, planning, neighbourhood/community leaders and local market experts (for example, estate agents). Focus groups were carried out with residents to tease out the degree of integration and the reasons for the evidence found on the ground about relative segregation vis-à-vis integration. Further details are given in Appendix 5 of this report.

Case study areas

Werrington, Peterborough

Werrington is a mixed-tenure 'township' in Peterborough. Construction began in the 1970s and was finished in the late 1980s. One characteristic of Werrington that differs from the earlier townships was that its development during the Thatcher years meant that its social mix philosophy was diluted.

Werrington Village has been in existence since the 17th century. New Werrington was developed around the village to the north of Peterborough as part of the wider New Town programme (a Mark III New Town designated in 1971) with an emphasis on owner-occupation. The township added to existing linked settlements and was intended to build 3,000 homes. Council planning figures suggest that, from 1980 to 1988, more than 3,100 buildings were constructed, 550 more from 1988 to 1991 and 179 from 1991 to 1997. The settlement has grown from less than 6,000 people in 1981 to just under 15,000 in 2000 (current Peterborough Council population is 156,050). It is noteworthy that in the 1980s around 700 units of new build were social renting and a further 489 were shared ownership with the balance of just under 2,000 either new for sale or council house sales. The planners' perspective is that Werrington is now largely built out and is approaching the capacity of its infrastructure.

About 10% of households are ethnic minorities in Peterborough but this is true of less than 5% in Werrington (2000 figures). However, the Peterborough Development Corporation (PDC) was also to provide social housing with incentives to buy at affordable prices, for instance, for key workers. A combination of the emphasis on owner-occupation and the subsequent Right-to-Buy scheme has resulted in a very low level of social housing in the area today. In 1988, PDC transferred its own social housing stock (about 7,000 units) – most of it to the council and about one in seven units to housing associations. However, recently, Peterborough Council transferred its stock to Cross Key Homes (a Registered Social Landlord) who today manage around 250 units in the Werrington area.

The area has maintained its village centre and the newer part has been built in avenues, cul-de-sacs and a street design that gives the feeling of smaller clusters of housing. Moreover, the properties are diverse and of different sizes and shapes. There are large green areas throughout including a lake that was developed by the PDC on request. The area is well maintained and there were no visible signs of any very run-down parts. Local groups are extremely active in the community, for instance, removing graffiti and collecting litter on a weekly basis.

In terms of social mix questions, this case study is relevant as an explicit planned tenure mix, with Werrington designed with blocks of PDC housing located within predominantly owner-occupied developments. The broad initial tenure mix – 80% owner-occupied (including shared ownership and cheaper starter homes) and 20% social rented – was unique in Peterborough. Today, social housing only accounts for around 10% of Werrington's housing stock. The change in tenure share is largely due to upmarket new build in recent years and the long-term erosion of social housing caused by the Right-to-Buy. Currently, the main housing policy issues concern the local low-wage economy, affordable housing and high levels of housing demand (across all tenures), and the possible use of Section 106 agreements to provide new affordable housing.

Newbiggin Hall, Newcastle-upon-Tyne

Newbiggin Hall was a peripheral single-tenure council estate built to the north of Newcastle as a response to slum clearance in the 1960s. The estate is based within the Woolsington ward (comprising 85% of the ward's population in 2002) and is built on the site of the 18th-century Newbiggin Hall and its surrounds. Woolsington lost 34% of its population between 1971 and 1998. When the estate was built, a large proportion of the new residents were families with children requiring two substantial schools. There is also a large proportion of residents aged 50+ (around 2,500). The council estimated that in 2002 the estate had around 2,500 dwellings. It was a typical large council estate with a large number of two- and three-bedroom houses, Dutch bungalows and three storey flats. During the 1980s, it was evident that it had become very run down, with increased social problems. After suffering accumulating problems of declining demand, management and housing quality problems, bids were made for large-scale regeneration, eventually securing SRB 4 funding in the mid-1990s.

Before the SRB programme there were around 2,500 units. Completed in the late 1990s, the SRB programme's physical redevelopment of the area involved demolition (particularly of the three-storey flats), and refurbishment to let and for sale. In addition, the project saw private sector new build, shared ownership and Registered Social Landlord development of bungalows. Much of the 150 or so for sale new build took place on adjacent greenfield sites rather than recycling land cleared by demolition.

Newbiggin Hall is a big estate with two definable communities who are relatively detached from each other. The estate has two primary schools and an unattractive 1970s shopping centre – retail did not get funded in the SRB programme in this case (although it was part of the master plan). Most people use the relatively good transport links to shop elsewhere.

The relevance as a case study is that this area's regeneration introduced lower cost owner-occupation (and, indeed, family and higher value owner occupation) into predominantly social housing areas in the mid-1990s. The housing market in Newbiggin Hall appears strong with evidence of former residents returning to the area, buyers trading up within the area and rising house prices. The resale market appears to be buoyant. At the same time, social renting demand is strong.

Hulme, Manchester

Hulme is a nationally well-known example of area decline and regeneration. Indeed, it is an area that has been heavily evaluated and researched (JRF, 1994; Harding, 1997; SURF Centre, 2002; Perry and Harding, 2003). Located off-centre in Manchester, Hulme constituted around 6,000 council homes with major social, economic, demand and physical problems. Manchester captured £37.5 million of City Challenge funding in the early 1990s, levering in private finds and redeveloping Hulme as a diverse, mixed-tenure project involving stock transfer to RSLs and private sector new build also.

City Challenge ran to 1997 but it has been estimated that a further £400 million was invested in the area from public and private sectors after 1997. Compared to 1992, by 2002 there had been a dramatic diversification of the housing stock, although nearly two in three households remain in social renting (SURF Centre, 2002). However, all sectors, including the rental market, are represented in Hulme. Demand is perceived to be strong with population increasing relative to the city average. It has achieved a high leverage ratio of approximately 6.7:1 (Harding, 1997).

During the City Challenge phase, the estate's housing was comprehensively redeveloped, reducing the tenure share from more than 90% council to just 44% by 1997 with 20% RSL, 25% private owner and 11% private rental housing. The development programme involved:

- 3,016 unfit council homes were demolished;
- 38% of the remaining council stock was improved;
- 1,111 new RSL units built;
- 214 private units built with plans implemented for a further 1,374 after 1997;
- 564 student rental flats; and
- 48 standard private rental.

Currently, social housing demand is high, the private housing market is working well and popular perceptions of the area have been significantly altered. Hulme is heterogeneous, comprising stable demand residents who have lived in the community a long time, including younger households now setting up home independently. At the same time, however, parts of the estate have acquired a trendy bohemian reputation oriented around cultural activities. The importance of cultural activities was, of course, noted in the previous chapter of this report. Students also feature strongly in the area. Hulme now makes more effective use of its accessibility to the city centre. Of course, this diversity can cause conflict but it is in the context of a vibrant neighbourhood and one with a generally healthy housing market.

According to the Centre for Sustainable Urban and Regional Forms (SURF Centre, 2002), the area remains a relatively poor one, with a disproportionately large share of transient households but also with large and increasing property values, Hulme is attracting professional and managerial households, which is also forcing local people to look elsewhere to buy. The centre concluded that the population in Hulme is more fragmented and less stable than would have been hoped for.

Hulme is an interesting case study, because it can examine the longer-run effects of the City Challenge programme in terms of explicit social and tenure mix – in this case, on a large scale, within one of England's major cities. Like Newbiggin Hall, Hulme's regeneration was about introducing home ownership into social housing areas, but in this case we have a longer period of time to test the research questions and, also, Hulme is, in its own right, idiosyncratic and heterogeneous.

The evidence

Werrington

The sustainability of an area over time, even in largely favourable circumstances, will be subject to external and internal drivers. In Werrington's case, the long-term effects of a large owner-occupied sector and the RTB have eroded the social housing stock. Externally, the wider house price inflation in the region has made housing less affordable for first-time buyers, putting pressure on the market and of course further incentivising tenants to exercise the RTB. Werrington has a relatively large amount of extensions that may represent lack of trading-up opportunities, affordability problems or, indeed, satisfaction with the neighbourhood. Werrington is a stable area – people tend to move in and stay, only perhaps moving within the area. For instance, owners interviewed had largely moved in when young for work, raised families and remained there. It was generally seen as a good area of Peterborough to live in. There is low turnover of housing association stock and indicators, generally, of strong demand for social housing. However, the interviews suggest a strong sense of community and pride in the local area; with community members active in the housing association and evidence of local councillors playing a large role in community life.

All the evidence suggests that tenants are fully embedded in the life of the community. Conflict is limited and what exists tends to be between residents in the old village and the New Town and also between younger and older social tenants There are issues of antisocial behaviour, although they are not a huge problem, arising from the lack of facilities for younger people. There is also evidence of feelings of isolation for some older people in the community.

Table 8.1 sets out the proportion of social rented housing in the two Census years of 1991 and 2001 for Werrington and the other case study areas. The table again shows that Werrington is a strongly owner-occupied area, with only approximately 10% of households in the social rented sector, compared with more than 20% for Peterborough as a whole in 2001. Furthermore, there has been almost no change in the share since 1991. This supports the view that Werrington is a very stable community, where social housing has made few inroads over the 10-year period. As noted

Table 8.1: The share of social housing in the case study areas

	Mean (%)		Standard Deviation	
	1991	2001	1991	2001
Werrington	10.56	10.66	18.63	18.50
Hulme	93.82	65.18	5.66	31.59
Woolsington (Newbiggin Hall)	63.48	49.03	35.25	28.31

earlier in this chapter, most of the new building was completed before 1991. However, averages do not tell the full story. Tenure mix and segregation are concerned with the *dispersion* of households within the overall area. Table 8.1, therefore, also sets out the standard deviation of the social rented share, calculated over the smallest spatial units available from each census, that is Output Areas (OAs) for 2001 and Enumeration Districts (EDs) for 1991. Although the two sets of areas are not entirely compatible, the general message that comes through is unlikely to be distorted. Not only are the averages very similar between the two years, but so also are the standard deviations. The social mixing appears to have changed little over the past 10 years.

This is reinforced by Figure 8.1. In the graphs, the social renting share is shown for each ED in Werrington in 1991 (left-hand graph) and OA in 2001 (right-hand graph). In the graphs, the ward average share is subtracted from each observation. This is in order to standardise for changes across time and across location. For example, the overall share will have fallen over time because of Right-to-Buy (RTB) sales. Furthermore, the subtraction of the average makes it easier to make comparisons with the other two case study areas. The EDs and OAs are then ranked according to the social rented shares from lowest to highest and plotted in the graphs. In an extreme case, if the graph were horizontal at a value of 0, this would imply that all OAs (EDs) had the same social rental share (and the standard deviation would also be 0). However, as the graph becomes steeper, this indicates a higher level of segregation of social tenants between the areas.

The patterns of the figures are remarkably similar between the two years. Most OAs (and EDs) have very small amounts of social housing, but a few, small areas have high proportions. Two OAs in 2001 have social housing shares greater than 65%. However, these only account for 177 households or less than 3% of the total number of households in Werrington. Six OAs have social housing shares lying between 45% and 65%. By contrast, 14 OAs have no social housing and 31 out of 50 have shares of less than 5%. The case study interviews indicate a high level of satisfaction with the area, but it would be hard to conclude that Werrington now demonstrates characteristics of a mixed community. The area has converged over time to one in which owner-occupation dominates in almost all areas and this has been the case for the past 10 years. Arguably, the original target of 20%

Figure 8.1: The social renting shares in Werrington (1991 and 2001)

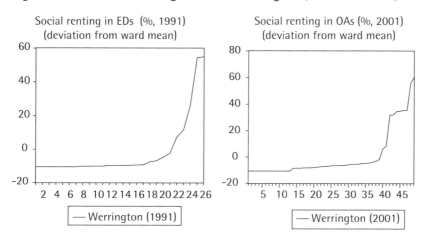

social housing, when the New Town began, was insufficient to be sustainable. The small proportion of social tenants is concentrated on a relatively small number of locations. There is little evidence from Werrington that mixing adds to satisfaction.

Newbiggin Hall

The interviews suggested that the phased redevelopment of the area in smaller parcels was successful both in terms of the management of decanting and in the introduction of new tenures. Smaller-scale developments allowed time for the area to adjust. For instance, bungalows were built by Nomad Housing for older residents relocated from the flats (having lived on the estate since it was built).

The success of home ownership in the area tapped into unmet demand and allowed households to trade up within the area, and for people with family connections there to move back into Newbiggin Hall. Initial objections by the private developer to building larger three-bedroom houses, due to perceived lack of demand, led to a fairly conservative two-year programme agreed for building on demand. In reality, the programme was finished and all houses sold within six months. People who had moved within or back to the area to starter homes were staying and in time wanted to buy larger homes. Prices of starter homes within the area have increased by around 50%, with a large number of residents 'staircasing up' through shared ownership schemes. A feature of the success of the insertion of home ownership has been growing take-up under the RTB scheme.

Interviews suggested that in comparison to the early stages of the regeneration programme, the success of the project has made it difficult to sustain community interest in the programme – the solving of key problems has returned many activists to their former lives.

The estate was redeveloped through the SRB 4 Programme, which included not only housing but also a wider economic and social programme, reinforcing the property-led dimensions of the project. Local groups and the community were active and closely involved at the consultative and development stages of the project. Managed by the North West Partnership, management was seen as a contributor to success due to the way the regeneration was tackled; that is, smaller-scale gradual developments, a mixture of appropriate housing, the tackling of wider social issues and looking at the needs of the estate rather than the requirements of the council. Other areas of Newcastle saw large-scale demolitions and private developments, which were less successful than in the case study.

Social rented demand is strong by all normal indicators (for example, voids, housing register, low turnover, demand from outside the area). There are problems of antisocial behaviour, although these are perceived to have fallen recently. The establishment of the county's police headquarters just on the edge of the estate has meant an increase in the number of police cars driving through the area and staff on the beat (as well as creating jobs and reducing the fear of crime).

Sustainability issues remain regarding the quality of local shopping and crystallising the plans to bring new retail to the estate. Although peripheral to Newcastle, the area is quite well linked by roads to the nearby airport and other sources of jobs. As the majority of residents are social tenants, economic regeneration will continue to play a key role in sustaining and defending investment. Social mix and the wider impact of a minority home ownership sector may in the end be subordinate to the social and economic success of social housing within Newbiggin Hall.

A resident focus group produced interesting findings:

- Different levels of awareness about social problems in the area, and to some degree evidence of isolation, is partly the result of housing design (bungalows with high fences around them for elderly social housing tenants). However, it should be pointed out that the bungalows' residents were very happy with their housing and immediate 'cocooned' environment.

- A strong sense of gradations of acceptability for different parts of the estate exists.
- The existence of young, bored people on the estate reflected a lack of organised activities.
- A recognition that many local shops had gone under (there is a local supermarket, however), but transport links to the city centre and shopping facilities were generally good.
- Although the community centre had been burned down there was a strong sense of community, as described by gala days, long-term residents socialising and local school and play parks being well used; there is also a local social club and a community centre (that particularly appeals in the evening to older residents). The older residents, however, contended that there was a greater sense of community when they first arrived.

Objective indicators of the changing patterns of segregation can, again, be derived from the Censuses. Table 8.1 shows a fall in the share of social housing from 63% to 49% as a result of the factors discussed earlier in this chapter. This is clearly a significant change. Figure 8.2 also indicates a changing distribution. Across the EDs in Woolsington in 1991, only five (out of 19) had a social rental share of less than 10%; 10 had shares greater than 70%. However, at the other extreme, three EDs had owner-occupation rates greater than 90%. By 2001, only five (out of 27) OAs had social shares greater than 70%. However, perhaps more importantly, a distinguishing feature of the change is that the rise in ownership has not been confined to a small number of locations. Although the distribution is certainly far from equal (the graph is quite steep) and eight OAs now have ownership rates greater than 60%, there are no areas in which ownership is entirely absent.

On the face of it, this appears to be a success story in terms of developing social mix. However, there are reasons to be cautious. Werrington suggested a stable community over, at least, a 10-year period, dominated by ownership. Arguably, in Newbiggin Hall, a community still in transition is observed. As described earlier in this chapter, policy action took place primarily under the SRB from the mid-1990s. These are early days in which to judge the long-run trend. It is still possible that the ward could tip in either direction.

Hulme

Hulme has been a totemic success story at least in terms of the physical regeneration of an infamous area into what is now a mixed-tenure fashionable area. While not all of its social and economic problems have been eradicated, nor indeed have all questions for the future been resolved, there is no doubt that the City Challenge project and further area-based assistance has transformed Hulme. The project has been a comprehensive regeneration in which housing played a major but only partial role – new public spaces, social facilities, economic development and job creation, all have also been important.

Figure 8.2: The social renting shares in Woolsington (1991 and 2001)

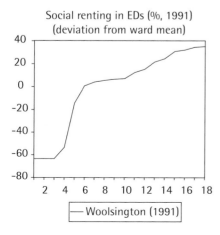

There is a strategic crunch facing the area between the regeneration goals of making Hulme family-friendly and socially stable or strengthening what it seems to be doing well – constructing a varied cosmopolitan, but transitional (in terms of residents) vibrant area. Arguably, the latter is necessary for cities to thrive. However, can it achieve both? The future of the project also has to wrestle with other problems, for instance, how to balance competing demands for land use, for example, housing versus commercial demands?

The area now enjoys high demand for social housing on normal indicators (voids, turnover, local versus wider demand, housing waiting lists) and lively active community participation. A combination of both process and development strategies in Hulme have led to more recent building in the form of high density flats, which are not ideal for families, but (international experience suggests) are important for attracting young, high-income, small households without children. Redevelopment led to decanted residents choosing new developments where they could remain with the same neighbours – reflecting the stability of the long-term residents.

Perry and Harding (2003) argue that Hulme is polarised between the life chances of private sector owner residents and those in social renting. There are huge contrasts between the resources and opportunities of social tenants relative to owners and indeed the students living in Hulme. Heterogeneity and diversity may be viewed positively in some respects, particularly as a source of longer-term urban dynamism, but it may serve to magnify social inequity and division and hence conflict.

This last conclusion is reinforced by Census data. Table 8.1 shows the very low standard deviation of the social rental share in 1991, that is almost all households were in this sector in every ED. This also shows up in Figure 8.3, where the graph is generally very flat. In one sense, there was very little tenure segregation at the time – almost all households in the area were in the same tenure. This illustrates the difference between segregation and deprivation. In Werrington, there was also a low degree of segregation because most households were in owner-occupation. The difference between the two case study areas is the level of deprivation. Segregation per se is not seen as a problem.

By 2001, the curve is noticeably steeper, demonstrating more diversity in Hulme. However, there is a step change in the graph. The social share in the 12th highest ranked OA is 73%, but only 48% in the 11th highest. Furthermore, it remains the case that 22 of the 33 OAs have social renting shares in excess of 70%. Therefore, in terms of tenure mix, care has to be taken. The changes since 1991 have not been distributed equally – change has been unbalanced. On this measure, segregation has actually increased over time, even if the level of poverty has fallen.

Figure 8.3: The social renting shares in Hulme (1991 and 2001)

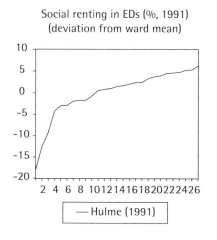

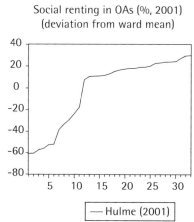

Cross-cutting conclusions

How did these three communities become mixed? We have seen that the case studies experienced different forms of policy intervention based on thoroughgoing development and redevelopment. We can contrast the careful master planning of a New Town township with community-involved regeneration programmes in two mono-tenure problem estates. However, despite the individual case studies being viewed as successful in terms of redevelopment and becoming thriving areas, the extent to which the neighbourhoods are truly mixed remains questionable. Owner-occupied housing is the dominant tenure in Werrington as a result of the cumulative effect of specific policies that guided its development. The remaining two case studies can be viewed as successful in terms of local indicators, but the communities that exist within each area remain substantially separate.

What factors explain the case study experience? First, local and wider contextual drivers are important, for instance, a lack of affordable house prices in surrounding areas. Second, the compositional characteristics of residents and the impact of succeeding generations also matter. This is clearly demonstrated in the case study areas where individuals have remained as neighbours or members of localised communities for a significant period of time and consequently a strong sense of community has developed. Third, purely neighbourhood effects are significant, such as the provision of local facilities and softer forms of regular interaction between different social groups through local schools, shopping and immediate neighbour relations. Fourth, each example relied on specific policy initiatives.

How sustainable are these examples and can we identify critical drivers and/or causes of non-sustainability? In all three cases, the estates are well connected to the wider metropolitan areas and these wider aspects are clearly essential to the well-being of any area. Hulme also raises the possibility that too much diversity may be a problem, although cultural diversity and dynamism may in the end be essential for the long-term survival of such an area within Greater Manchester, even if that is to the detriment of some more established residents who live there. However, it should be emphasised that the patterns described in this chapter are probably not the final outcomes that will emerge over time. Arguably only Werrington is in a stable state, dominated by owner-occupied housing. As we have noted in earlier chapters of this report, the theoretical literature suggests that segregated outcomes are likely to be the norm. Consequently, the more diverse patterns that have emerged so far in Hulme and Newbiggin Hall may turn out to be temporary outcomes in response to relatively recent policy initiatives – a phase transition in the jargon[1]. Over time, they may tip towards much higher levels of owner-occupation or back towards reliance on the social sector. It would be dangerous to predict which. However, the point is that, because we now observe more owning than 10 years ago, it cannot be concluded that these communities will be permanently mixed.

What broader lessons does this stage of the work have for the project as a whole? First, well-planned, durable and *large-scale* interventions are required to have the kinds of impacts we have seen. The interventions have to be large enough to allow areas to reach a take-off point. Second, temporal and group dynamics are important to help understand neighbourhood processes. Analysis needs to be sufficiently aware of cohort effects, for instance, of young households, forming families, requiring schooling, empty-nesting and then ageing and how the local community's degree of 'mixed-ness' has to retain the flexibility required to work for each of these different life-cycle stages. At the same time, wider economic forces, external drivers, operating at larger scales are clearly also important. Long-term sustainability will depend on how successful private markets for owner-occupation coexist with high demand social renting and whether the latter can fend off erosion from the RTB and at the same time defend investment.

---

[1] Hulme in Figure 8.3 for 2001 looks rather like the phase transition or threshold of Figure 3.1. At a particular point, owner-occupation takes off.

9

Golden rules for developing mixed communities

As discussed in Chapter 3 of this report, attempts to achieve mixed communities are not new, even though they remain at the heart of government policy today. Our brief literature review indicates that we should not expect mixing to be a panacea. The distinction has to be made between improvements to the external image of an estate and the internal social dynamics. The perception might well be that mixed tenure reduces the stigma of the most deprived areas, but there is little evidence of a transformation of the social dynamics. There is also little evidence of social mixing among the tenure groups and the neighbourhood may be more of a focus of social relationships for renters than for owners, whose social activities are concentrated outside the area.

Nevertheless, in Europe and the US, a wide variety of programmes have been adopted. These can broadly be characterised into three types:

- Revitalisation programmes designed to make neighbourhoods more attractive to middle-class households.
- Programmes designed to move low-income households to better-off neighbourhoods.
- Subsidies to moderate-income households in order to persuade them to live in the worst neighbourhoods.

The first of these is sometimes taken as the European model (see Skifter Andersen, 2002), whereas the second and third, through voucher schemes, have been more common in the US. Vouchers give greater choice to individuals, but, arguably, production subsidies are better suited to achieving targeted neighbourhood revitalisation. Schill et al (2002) argue that New York's 10-year revitalisation programme produced positive spillovers onto neighbouring areas in terms of raising property prices. The US Gautreaux and Moving to Opportunity Programmes are the best-known examples of attempts to move low-income households to better neighbourhoods. By contrast, Nehemiah developments are attempts to provide below-cost homes, in areas of high poverty, to moderate-income groups, who are becoming owners for the first time. Therefore, these groups gain from becoming owners, but suffer from greater exposure to areas of high crime and poor schooling (see Cummings et al, 2002).

Based on the analysis of the earlier chapters, a set of conditions for the development of mixed communities can be suggested. These arise directly from our empirical results:

1. Any policy must enable the neighbourhood to reach the take-off point. Otherwise private sector support will not be forthcoming either through development activities or through an increase in owner-occupation. Above the threshold, the returns are too low to be attractive, including the capital gains on owner-occupation. Since deprivation is strongly related to local unemployment and long-term illness, any policy almost certainly needs to reduce these significantly. However, there is only a limited amount the local authority can do. A reduction in deprivation needs vibrant national, regional and local economies and an improvement in the local skills base. Therefore, area policies need to go hand-in-hand with labour market policies.

The former support the latter in order to dissuade those whose skills improve from leaving the most deprived areas.

2. One-size-fits-all policies do not work. Spatial targeting is necessary.

3. Big projects have a greater impact than a series of smaller projects. However, the cost will be high. Of the case studies, Hulme is a good example, although Newbiggin Hall reports benefits from a phased approach.

4. Traditional evaluation techniques would produce the highest returns by targeting projects in areas close to the threshold. Measured returns will be much lower in areas of high deprivation. However, this is a criticism of the evaluation techniques, not of the need for expenditures in areas of high deprivation.

5. Incentives should be targeted on those most likely to move into the area, that is the young and highly skilled without children. The probability of attracting back older households who have already left urban areas is much lower, at least up to retirement age, although the moving decisions of 'empty nesters' have not been explored here. This suggests that *initially* cultural and sporting facilities should receive special attention. Hulme, again, is a case in point, although this emphasis can lead to more transient populations. The evidence presented here on the effect of school quality on location choices for movers is inconclusive. This is, clearly, highly controversial. The traditional view is that school quality is critical to location. Furthermore, by concentrating resources on richer groups, it is regressive. The gains to existing residents only accrue indirectly as the local tax base rises and area quality improves. However, few migrants will be attracted to areas of very high unemployment.

6. The local authority needs to decide whether its optimal long-term strategy is to retain the 'newcomers' at a later stage of their life cycles or accept their loss and target the next cohort of the young. If the former is the aim, the advantage is that networks improve with length of residency, but the authority will, then, have to provide high quality schools and other elements of infrastructure to retain the migrants as they have children. Although not part of our study, the evidence suggests that school quality is crucial in retaining residents.

7. Even more controversially, there may be a case for providing council tax discounts or other tax subsidies for high-skilled potential residents (see Meen and Andrew, 2004). Fiscal policy has been underused, but the results indicate that high council taxes discourage migrants. Again, this is regressive.

8. Even if there is an observed need, do not build more social housing in the most deprived areas. Currently most social house building takes place in areas where the social stock is largest. However, this simply concentrates deprivation and segregation further.

References

Abraham, J.M. and Hendershott, P.H. (1996) 'Bubbles in Metropolitan Housing Markets', *Journal of Housing Research*, vol 7, no 2, pp 191-207.

Abramson, A.J., Tobin, M.S. and VanderGoot, M.R. (1995) 'The Changing Geography of Metropolitan Opportunity: The Segregation of the Poor in US Metropolitan Areas, 1970 to 1990', *Housing Policy Debate*, vol 6, no 1, pp 45-72.

Allen, C., Camina, M., Casey, R., Coward, S. and Wood, M. (2005) *Nothing Out of the Ordinary: Mixed Tenure, Twenty Years On*, York: JRF.

Andersson, R. and Bråmå, A. (2004) 'Selective Migration in Swedish Distressed Neighbourhoods: Can Area-Based Urban Policies Counteract Segregation Processes?' *Housing Studies*, vol 19, no 4, pp 517-40.

Atkinson, R. and Kintrea, K. (2000) 'Owner-Occupation, Social Mix and Neighbourhood Impacts', *Policy and Politics*, vol 28, pp 93-108.

Bailey, N. and Pickering, J. (2004) 'Deprived Areas and Deprived Individuals: Understanding the Relationship', Paper presented to the European Network for Housing Research Conference, University of Cambridge, July.

Beroube, A. (2005) *Mixed Communities in England: A US Perspective on Evidence and Policy Prospects*, York: Joseph Rowntree Foundation.

Bolster, A., Burgess, S., Johnson, R., Jones, K., Propper, C. and Starker, R. (2004) *Neighbourhoods, Households and Income Dynamics: A Semi-Parametric Investigation of Neighbourhood Effects*, Bristol: Department of Economics, University of Bristol.

Crow, G. and Allan, G. (1994) *Community Life: An Introduction to Local Social Relations*, London: Harvester Wheatsheaf.

Cummings, J.L., DiPasquale, D. and Kahn, M.E. (2002) 'Measuring the Consequences of Promoting Inner City Homeownership', *Journal of Housing Economics*, vol 11, pp 330-59.

Cutler, D.M., Glaeser, E.L. and Vigdor, J.L. (1999) 'The Rise and Decline of the American Ghetto', *Journal of Political Economy*, vol 107, no 3, pp 455-506.

DETR (2000) *Regeneration that Lasts*, London: The Stationery Office.

Dorling, D. and Rees, P. (2003) 'A Nation Still Dividing: The British Census and Social Polarisation 1971-2001', *Environment and Planning A*, vol 35, pp 1287-313.

Egan, J. (2004) *The Egan Review: Skills for Sustainable Communities*, London: Office of the Deputy Prime Minister.

Englund, P. and Ioannides, Y. (1997) 'House Price Dynamics: An International Empirical Perspective', *Journal of Housing Economics*, vol 6, no 2, pp 119-36.

Friedrichs, J. (1996) 'Context Effects of Poverty Neighbourhoods on Residents', Keynote Address, European Network of Housing Research Conference, Copenhagen.

Galster, G.C. (2002) 'An Economic Efficiency Analysis of Deconcentrating Poverty Populations', *Journal of Housing Economics*, vol 11, pp 303-29.

Granovetter, M. (1972) 'The Strength of Weak Ties', *American Journal of Sociology*, vol 78, pp 1360-80.

Green, A.E. (1994) *The Geography of Poverty and Wealth*, Warwick: Institute for Employment Research, University of Warwick.

Harding, A. (1997) *Hulme City Challenge: Did It Work?*, Manchester: SURF Centre, University of Salford.

Johnston, R., Forrest, J. and Poulsen, M. (2002) 'Are There Ethnic Enclaves/Ghettos in English Cities?', *Urban Studies*, vol 39, no 4, pp 591-618.

JRF (Joseph Rowntree Foundation) (1994) *Lessons from Hulme. Housing Summary Findings 5*, September, York: JRF.

Kintrea, K., Gibb, K., Keoghan, M., Munro, M., McGregor, A. and Hermansen, C. (1996) *An Evaluation of GRO Grants for Owner-Occupation*, Edinburgh: Scottish Office.

Kleinhans, R. (2004) 'Social Implications of Housing Diversification in Urban Renewal: A Review of Recent Literature', *Journal of Housing and the Built Environment*, vol 19, pp 367-90.

Kling, J., Ludwig, J. and Katz, L. (2005) 'Neighbourhood Effects on Crime for Female and Male Youth: Evidence from a Randomised Housing Voucher Experiment', *Quarterly Journal of Economics*, vol 120, pp 87-130.

Krugman, P. (1996) *The Self-Organizing Economy*, Oxford: Blackwells.

Martin, G. and Watkinson, J. (2003) 'Rebalancing Communities by Mixing Tenure on Social Housing Estates', *Joseph Rowntree Foundation Findings 523*, May, York: JRF.

Massey, D. and Denton, N.A. (1988) 'Suburbanization and Segregation in US Metropolitan Areas', *American Journal of Sociology*, vol 94, pp 592-626.

Meen, D. and Meen, G. (2003) 'Social Behaviour as a Basis for Modelling the Urban Housing Market: A Review', *Urban Studies*, vol 40, pp 917-35.

Meen, G. (2001) *Modelling Spatial Housing Markets: Theory, Analysis and Policy*, Boston: Kluwer Academic Publishers.

Meen, G. (2002) 'The Time Series Behavior of House Prices: A Transatlantic Divide?', *Journal of Housing Economics*, vol 11, pp 1-23.

Meen, G. (2004a) 'Non-Linear Behaviour in Local Housing Markets and the Implications for Sustainable Mixed-Income Communities in England', Paper presented to the ENHR Conference, University of Cambridge, July.

Meen, G. (2004b) 'Home-Ownership Sustainability: Concepts and Measurement', Mimeo, Prepared for the Joseph Rowntree Foundation Home Ownership Inquiry: 2010 and Beyond.

Meen, G. and Andrew, M. (2004) 'On the Use of Policy to Reduce Housing Market Segmentation', *Regional Science and Urban Economics*, vol 34, pp 727-51.

Montgomery, J. (1994) 'Weak Ties, Employment and Inequality: An Equilibrium Analysis', *American Journal of Sociology*, vol 99, pp 1212-36.

NRU (Neighbourhood Renewal Unit) (2002) *The National Strategy for Neighbourhood Renewal. Fact Sheet No 2*, (www.neighbourhood.gov.uk/publications.asp?did=154).

ODPM (Office of the Deputy Prime Minister) (2003) *Sustainable Communities: Building for the Future*, London: ODPM.

ODPM (2005a) *Sustainable Communities: Homes for All*, Cm 6424, London: ODPM.

ODPM (2005b) *Sustainable Communities: People, Places and Prosperity*, Cm 6425, London: ODPM.

Oreopolous, P. (2003) 'The Long Run Consequences of Living in a Poor Neighbourhood', *Quarterly Journal of Economics*, vol 118, pp 1533-75.

Parkinson, M. (1998) *Combating Social Exclusion: Lessons from Area-Based Programmes in Europe*, Bristol: The Policy Press.

Perry, E. and Harding, A. (2003) 'Off the critical list', *New Start*, 24 January, p 14.

Power, A. and Mumford, K. (1999) *The Slow Death of Great Cities*, York: JRF.

Robson, B., Parkinson, M., Boddy, M. and Maclennan, D. (2000) *The State of English Cities*, London: DETR.

Schelling, T. (1971) 'Dynamic Models of Segregation', *Journal of Mathematical Sociology*, vol 1, pp 143-86.

Schill, M.H, Ellen, I.G., Schwartz, A.E. and Voicu, I. (2002) 'Revitalizing Inner-City Neighborhoods: New York City's Ten-Year Plan', *Housing Policy Debate*, vol 13, no 3, p 529-66.

Skifter Andersen, H. (2002) 'Can Deprived Housing Areas Be Revitalised? Efforts Against Segregation and Neighbourhood Decay in Denmark and Europe', *Urban Studies*, vol 39, no 4, p 767-90.

SURF Centre (Centre for Sustainable Urban and Regional Forms) (2002) *Hulme, Ten Years On: Report to Manchester City Council*, Manchester: SURF Centre, University of Salford.

Tunstall, R. (2002) 'The Promotion of Mixed Tenure: In Search of the Evidence Base', Paper presented at the Housing Studies Association Conference, York, Spring (www.york.ac.uk/inst/chp/hsa/papers/spring2002.htm).

Wilcox, S. (2003) *Can Work – Can't Buy: Local Measures of the Ability of Working Households to Become Home Owners*, York: JRF.

Wilson, W. (1987) *The Truly Disadvantaged: The Inner City, the Underclass and Public Policy*, Chicago, IL: University of Chicago Press.

Young, H.P. (1998) *Individual Strategy and Social Structure. An Evolutionary Theory of Institutions*, Princeton, NJ: Princeton University Press.

Appendix 1: Thresholds in local house prices

The theory underlying the model of local house prices is discussed in detail in Meen (2004). This develops a non-linear logistic function:

Equation 1

$$y_i = 1 - \frac{b_1}{1 + e^{(c_2 + c_3 IMD_i + c_4 (H/HH)_i + c_5 (INC)_i + \varepsilon_i)}} \tag{1}$$

y_i = local authority house prices relative to the maximum regional price in which the local authority exists

IMD = Index of Multiple Deprivation (relative to regional average)

H = number of owner-occupied dwellings

HH = number of households

INC = household income

i = a spatial subscript

In addition to the level of deprivation, the remaining regressors are, firstly, a supply-side measure of the owner-occupier housing stock. Meen (2002) demonstrates the substantial omitted variable biases that arise from the omission of the housing stock in price equations. However, rather than simply the housing stock, a better measure is the owner-occupier housing stock *per household*. This preserves homogeneity – a doubling of the housing stock and the number of households has no effect on prices. The second variable added is a measure of local household income, constructed by Wilcox (2003). It could be argued that income is already partly captured by the Deprivation Index but, in house price studies, income is consistently a very important variable and it is useful to test any additional contribution from this indicator.

Table 1.1a: Instrumental variable parameter estimates in the logistic house price equation (estimated over the English local authorities)

Area	b_1	c_2	c_3	c_4	c_5	R^2	SEE	Obsn
England (excluding London)	0.723 (imposed)	−0.307 (8.9)	−0.080 (13.4)	−0.034 (5.3)	7.38E-05 (8.7)	0.69	0.090	320
North	0.711 (imposed)	−0.564 (8.9)	−0.094 (10.1)	−0.041 (4.2)	5.11E-05 (2.1)	0.72	0.087	87
Midlands	0.723 (imposed)	−0.502 (6.8)	−0.101 (9.1)	−0.056 (3.8)	7.95E-05 (3.9)	0.81	0.071	74
South	0.685 (imposed)	−0.267 (5.3)	−0.090 (7.8)	−0.023 (2.5)	6.68E-05 (5.6)	0.68	0.089	159

t-values in brackets

North   = North East, North West, Yorkshire and Humberside
Midlands = East Midlands, West Midlands
South   = East, South East, South West
SEE   = equation standard error

The results of the model are presented in Table 1.1a. Regional as well as national results are given (that is estimated over all 353 local authorities). In the table, b_1 has been imposed. This ensures that prices vary between a minimum (non-0) value and a maximum of unity, since the average price of housing never falls to 0. Usually $b_1 = 0.723$, which implies that the *minimum* local authority house price is 27.7% of the regional maximum.

All the variables are highly significant and take their expected signs, including the housing supply variable. The coefficient on the dwelling stock is significantly negative. The regional equations provide stability tests and the stability of the deprivation coefficient is noteworthy. Slightly more variation in the responsiveness to income change is, however, evident.

The results in Table 1.1a concentrate on the *static* relationship between median prices in local authorities and measures of deprivation, income and housing supply. Given that consistent measures of the Deprivation Index – the key measure of human capital and neighbourhood conditions – are not available on a time-series basis, the emphasis is unsurprising. The variation in the sample is across space rather than time. Nevertheless we could consider the 'static' relationship as one measure of the 'fundamentals' towards which the market is adjusting. The deviation of prices (measured in 2001) from the fundamentals (in other words, the error term) could be considered as a measure of the extent of under- or overvaluation to be corrected in subsequent time periods.

However, given that we only have a measure of disequilibrium in one time period, full dynamic analysis is not possible. We consider, therefore, the dynamics of price change between 2001 and 2002. Following Abraham and Hendershott (1996), the model could be considered in terms of 'bubble builders' and 'bubble bursters', although there are other interpretations. A lagged dependent variable captures the former, whereas the disequilibrium term proxies the latter. The model could also be considered as a form of error correction process, although the limited nature of the time-series dynamics needs to be borne in mind. It would also be valuable to include other dynamic terms. However, at the local authority level, a limited choice of indicators is available. We have chosen to include the local unemployment rate, which is now available on a residence (rather than workplace) basis. Since unemployment was found to be the key determinant of deprivation, this is likely to be a good indicator of the dynamics of neighbourhood change.

Therefore the basic model takes the form of Equation 2:

Equation 2

$$\Delta \ln ph_i = a_1 + a_2 \Delta \ln ph_{i-1} + a_3 \Delta \ln ph_{reg} + a_4 \Delta up_i + a_5 diseq_{i-1} \tag{2}$$

where:

ph   = median house price
up   = unemployment rate
disequil = measure of disequilibrium derived as $\ln(ph/ph^*)$ and ph^* is the estimated value of prices taken from Table 1.1a.
Δ = measures the change between 2001 and 2002

i refers to the local authority
(reg) is the regional average

a_2 captures any autocorrelation in the price dynamics. There is considerable international evidence for this (see Englund and Ioannides, 1997), whereas a_5 captures the speed at which any disequilibrium is eliminated. Stability requires the coefficient to be negative. The regional average house price growth is included to capture any region-wide dynamics, affecting all local authorities equally. The first row of Table 1.2a gives the national results. The row indicates that: autocorrelation occurs, regional-wide influences are important, a rise in unemployment reduces price growth (although the term has a one period time lag), and approximately 10% of any disequilibrium was removed between 2001 and 2002. Remember that this cannot be interpreted in the conventional way. We cannot argue that 10% of the disequilibrium is eliminated each year since price change in only one year is being considered. Nevertheless, all the coefficients are in line with expectations and are significant.

Rows two to four disaggregate to the blocs of regions previously considered in Table 1.1a. If the ripple effect has statistical validity, we should *not* expect the coefficients to be the same since the South responds to shocks (and disequilibrium) before the North of England. Furthermore, between 2001 and 2002 price growth was very different between the North and South. Whereas prices in the South grew rapidly, the North registered more modest changes (although the pattern was reversed in 2003 and 2004).

In line with our priors, the fit of the equation is much better in the South in terms of R^2, equation standard error and significance of the individual coefficients. Approximately 15% of the disequilibrium was eliminated between the two time periods. However, in contrast, the equation explains very little of the price movements in the North and none of the coefficients are significant, except the disequilibrium term, which (against expectations) turns out to be *positive*. This implies that if, for example, local prices are below the level determined by fundamentals, they fell further in 2002. However, to emphasise the point, this does not generalise to all years, but reflects outcomes in one year and the fact that adjustment is slower in the North than in the South.

Table 1.2a: Dynamic house price models (2001–02). Dependent variable = $\Delta\ln(ph)$

Area	constant	$\Delta\ln(ph)_{-1}$	$\Delta\ln(ph)_{reg}$	Δup	Δup_{-1}	disequil	R^2	SEE
England (excluding London)	0.034 (1.7)	0.187 (2.6)	0.667 (6.5)	–	–0.047 (3.6)	–0.100 (3.2)	0.33	0.047
North	0.142 (2.0)	–0.016 (0.1)	0.242 (0.5)	0.080 (1.9)	0.064 (1.8)	0.204 (2.3)	0.20	0.057
Midlands	0.038 (0.6)	–	0.785 (2.2)	–	–0.069 (2.2)	–0.187 (2.6)	0.18	0.042
South (excluding London)	0.078 (4.3)	–	0.517 (6.2)	–0.086 (4.8)	–0.063 (3.9)	–0.152 (5.2)	0.57	0.031

t-values in brackets

Table 1.3a: Dynamic house price models (2002-03). Dependent variable = $\Delta\ln(ph)$

Area	constant	$\Delta\ln(ph)_{-1}$	$\Delta\ln(ph)_{reg}$	Δup	Δup_{-1}	disequil	R^2	SEE
England (excluding London)	0.049 (2.6)	0.157 (3.4)	0.538 (5.5)	–	-0.073 (5.4)	-0.046 (1.7)	0.36	0.042
North	0.063 (0.9)	–	0.728 (1.9)	–	–	-0.148 (2.0)	0.04	0.053
Midlands	-0.101 (1.8)	–	1.404 (5.1)	–	-0.073 (3.3)	-0.104 (1.9)	0.35	0.032
South (excluding London)	0.097 (5.9)	0.316 (3.9)	–	–	-0.080 (4.1)	0.049 (1.4)	0.37	0.036

t-values in brackets

The national equation includes a dummy for the North.

As an illustration, Table 1.3a considers price change between 2002 and 2003. The basic specification remains as in Equation 2, although the results omit insignificant variables. At the national level, the equation fit is marginally better, although the adjustment coefficient is weaker and the improvement comes primarily from the North. The fit is noticeably worse in the South and the adjustment coefficient is insignificant. However, the fit is better in the Midlands (although the adjustment coefficient is smaller). However, the key result is that, in the North, the adjustment coefficient now becomes significant and negative. The results are, therefore, consistent with the observed ripple effect.

Appendix 2: The determinants of gross migration flows

Table 2.1a: Gross migration flows in England

	Type of migration	Const.	IMD	% POP 16-24	% POP 25-29	OO	ΔUR	Comp/pop	VR	R²	SEE
North	In	7.339 (4.29)	-0.113 (10.78)	0.403 (5.89)	-0.417 (2.50)	-0.048 (2.79)			29.090 (3.73)	0.692	0.776
	Out	6.658 (4.09)	-0.095 (9.49)	0.285 (4.37)	-0.240 (1.51)	-0.046 (2.82)			33.911 (4.57)	0.629	0.737
Midlands	In	6.111 (2.13)	-0.106 (5.48)	0.491 (5.51)	-0.591 (3.05)	-0.037 (1.29)	-1.440 (2.11)	218.877 (4.03)	27.837 (2.06)	0.618	0.840
	Out	6.628 (2.86)	-0.078 (4.95)	0.414 (5.54)	-0.575 (3.57)	-0.024 (1.00)	-1.069 (1.83)			0.513	0.725
South excluding London	In	5.462 (3.54)	-0.105 (9.32)	0.325 (7.93)	-0.191 (2.84)	-0.027 (1.84)	-1.221 (3.10)	144.803 (3.50)	19.573 (2.45)	0.598	0.663
	Out	7.084 (5.20)	-0.127 (11.13)	0.243 (7.32)		-0.038 (2.67)	-0.862 (2.15)			0.668	0.683
London*	In	6.772 (3.44)	-0.135 (6.37)	0.117 (1.07)	0.566 (8.27)	-0.068 (4.08)	-1.625 (3.49)	116.594 (1.52)	-30.079 (2.24)	0.951	0.495
	Out	4.214 (2.19)	-0.112 (6.34)	0.178 (1.53)	0.567 (7.90)	-0.049 (2.93)	-2.027 (4.26)			0.947	0.530

* The City of London is excluded.

IMD	=	Index of Multiple Deprivation
UR	=	% of the population aged 16-74 who are unemployed
% POP 16-24	=	% of population aged 16-24
% POP 25-29	=	% of population aged 25-29
OO	=	owner-occupation rate
VR	=	vacancy rate
Comp/pop	=	number of housing completions per capita

Table 2.1a sets out the determinants of gross migration flows for the four regional blocs, estimated across the local authorities. Insignificant terms are eliminated from the equations. An alternative version of the equation set included local authority house prices relative to the regional maximum, that is the dependent variable in Equation 1 of Appendix 1. Although statistically significant, implying that high house prices generate net migration outflows, prices are strongly correlated with some of the variables in Table 2.1a. As a result, these other variables become less significant. Therefore, prices are excluded from this version in favour of the underlying determinants.

The results suggest that the key variables determining inflows and outflows from each local authority are the level of deprivation in the area (IMD), the proportion of the population in the 16-24 and 25-29 age groups (% POP 16-24, % POP 25-29), the owner-occupation rate (OO), the change in unemployment (ΔUR) and in some cases the level of housing completions relative to population (Comp/pop), and the vacancy rate (VR). As noted earlier, the last two sets of variables represent ways in which market equilibrium might be established following external shocks. By contrast, if flows are negatively related to deprivation, migration flows can reinforce patterns of deprivation and segregation over time.

Notice that, typically, each term has the same sign in both the inflows and outflows equations. An increase in deprivation, for example, both reduces inflows and outflows. The net effect on population flows depends, therefore, on the relative size of the coefficients. In many cases the absolute sizes are similar; therefore, a change in the determinants has large effects on the gross flows, but the net flows are smaller. Table 2.1a confirms that deprivation is a highly significant determinant of both inflows and outflows. Individuals do not wish to move to areas of high deprivation, but find it difficult to leave if they are already there. This will add to the cumulative processes of decline observed in the worst areas.

Young households in the 16-24 age group are particularly mobile, but mobility among the 25-29 age group is slightly more complex. Outside of London, the effects are negative, but, perhaps unsurprisingly, in London, the effects are positive. In line with conventional wisdom, areas with high owner-occupancy rates tend to experience low rates of moving and individuals are not attracted to areas of high unemployment.

Whereas the Deprivation Index is consistently highly significant across all regions, however, the effects of vacancies and housing availability are more spasmodic. The availability of new housing, in terms of completions, is important in the Midlands, the South and in London, although there is no significant effect in the North. In each case, the effects unsurprisingly are on inflows rather than outflows. Vacancies encourage both inflows and outflows in the North, but the coefficient on the latter is greater, suggesting that high levels of vacancies (which may reflect urban decline) generate net outflows. Therefore, in the North where supply is generally less of a constraint, this variable will contribute to cumulative processes of decline. In contrast, higher levels of vacancies generate inflows to the Midlands and South. In London, however, vacancies (again as a potential indicator of deprivation) reduce inflows.

In summary, a priori, there is a set of competing forces, some of which are stabilising to the local market in response to adverse shocks and some of which are destabilising. The overall effect can only be judged from simulation of the full model. However, the consistency and strength of the deprivation effects stand out.

In Table 2.1a, flows are related linearly to deprivation. However, from the arguments in the main text, the relationship may be non-linear. Therefore, the first two rows of Table 2.2a re-estimates the London equation adding squared and cubed to the equation. Comparing the London equations in the two tables, the fit improves. The non-linear functions are graphed in Figure 6.1, at the average values for the other variables.

The third and fourth rows consider the *wards* of Greater Manchester. Again non-linearity is important, although this is more significant in the outflows equation. The relationships between gross flows and deprivation are graphed in Figure 6.2 of the main text.

Table 2.2a: Gross migration flows – non-linear versions

	Type of migra-tion	Const.	IMD	IMD^2	IMD^3	% POP 16-24	% POP 25-29	OO	ΔUR	Comp/pop	R^2	SEE
London (boroughs)	In	5.942 (4.07)	-0.506 (6.01)	0.013 (4.80)	-0.00013 (4.71)	0.136 (1.57)	0.628 (11.07)	-0.034 (2.59)	-1.090 (3.01)	109.38 (1.80)	0.970	0.392
	Out	4.544 (2.45)	-0.334 (3.21)	0.0079 (2.27)	-7.71E-05 (2.32)	0.201 (1.84)	0.611 (8.54)	-0.036 (2.20)	-1.828 (4.01)		0.957	0.498
Greater Manchester (wards)	In	7.728 (4.77)	-0.198 (3.96)	0.0026 (1.93)	-2.01E-05 (1.83)	0.645 (25.20)	0.476 (6.98)	-0.094 (6.45)			0.912	1.215
	Out	7.950 (4.80)	-0.243 (4.75)	0.0038 (2.77)	-2.42E-05 (2.16)	0.499 (19.06)	0.521 (7.45)	-0.074 (4.97)			0.874	1.244

* The City of London is excluded.

Appendix 3:
The logit models of moving and location

Table 3.1a: Logit model estimating the probability that a household moves

	Coefficients	Z–Values
Constant	−0.664	1.99
Age 22-30	−0.530	1.75
Age 31-35	−1.108	3.37
Age 36-40	−1.415	4.21
Age 41+	−1.627	5.23
Self-employed	0.924	3.98
Professionals-Managers	0.723	3.85
Non-managers	0.524	3.43
Student-previous	1.468	4.98
Household-income	4.04E-06	1.05
Household-income (% change)	2.95E-04	2.04
Marital-change	0.729	2.97
Owner-occupier	−1.670	10.35
Social-renter	−0.755	4.53
Pseudo R²	0.156	

Key:

Age 22-30	Head of household is aged between 22-30
Age 31-35	Head of household is aged between 31-35
Age 36-40	Head of household is aged between 36-40
Age 41+	Head of household is aged 41 or over
Self-employed	Head of household is self-employed
Professionals-managers	Head of household is either a professional or a manager
Non-managers	Head of household works but is not a professional or manager
Student-previous	Head of household was a student in the previous wave
Household-income	Household income over the previous wave
Household-income (% change)	The change in household income between the current and previous wave
Marital-change	Change in marital status from the previous year
Owner-occupier	Household in owner-occupation
Social-renter	Household in social rental sector

Time and location dummy variables were found to be insignificant. The dependent variable takes a value of one if the household moves and zero otherwise.

Table 3.2a: Logit model estimating the probability that a household moved to a different TTWA

	Coefficients	Z-Values
Constant	0.390	0.26
Age 41+	−0.642	1.48
Student	−2.313	3.04
Degree	0.785	1.61
A-Level	1.796	2.90
Social-renter	−1.675	2.43
Move-job-reason	1.951	3.32
UpTTWA2001a	1.228	1.59
UpTTWA2001b	−0.831	1.07
IMD2004a	0.304	2.02
IMD2004b	−0.462	3.34
Pseudo R^2	0.512	

Key:

Age 41+	Head of household is aged 41 or over
Student	Head of household is a student
Degree	Head of household's highest qualification is a degree
A-Level	Head of household's highest qualification is an A-Level
Social-renter	Household in social rental sector
Move-job-reason	Moved for a job-related reason
UpTTWA2001a	Unemployment rate for the Travel to Work Area that households have moved from for 2001
UpTTWA2001b	Unemployment rate for the Travel to Work Area that households have moved to for 2001
IMD2004a	The level of deprivation for the area that households have moved from
IMD2004b	The level of deprivation for the area that households have moved to

Dependent variable takes a value of one if the household moves to a different TTWA.

Table 3.3a: Logit model estimating the probability that a household moved to a different local authority within the same TTWA

	Coefficients	Z-Values
Constant	2.361	0.54
Age 41+	−0.844	1.62
Children 5-15	−0.728	1.53
Marital-change	1.735	2.06
Move-job-reason	1.634	1.92
Culture1	−0.268	2.27
Culture2	0.212	1.79
Sport1	−0.281	1.99
Sport2	0.335	2.30
Council tax1	0.016	2.37
Council tax2	−0.019	2.81
GCSE1	0.497	2.91
GCSE2	−0.534	3.01
GCSEsd1	0.141	0.95
GCSEsd2	−0.088	0.58
Up2000a	6.915	3.83
Up2000b	−7.470	4.12
Dup2000a	5.365	3.26
Dup2000b	−5.686	3.35
Pseudo R^2	0.318	

Key:

Age 41+	Head of household is aged 41+
Children 5-15	Number of children aged 5-15
Marital-change	Change in marital status from the previous year
Move-job-reason	Moved for a job-related reason
Culture1	Satisfaction with cultural facilities in previous location
Culture2	Satisfaction with cultural facilities in current location
Sport1	Satisfaction with sporting facilities in previous location
Sport2	Satisfaction with sporting facilities in current location
Council tax1	Council tax for band D properties in previous location
Council tax2	Council tax for band D properties in current location
GCSE1	% obtaining 5 or more GCSEs grade A-C in previous location
GCSE2	% obtaining 5 or more GCSEs grade A-C in current location
GCSEsd1	Standard deviation of GCSE results across schools in previous location
GCSEsd2	Standard deviation of GCSE results across schools in current location
Up2000a	Unemployment rate for the LAD from which households have moved
Up2000b	Unemployment rate for the LAD to which households have moved
Dup2000a	Change in the unemployment rate for the LAD from which households have moved
Dup2000b	Change in the unemployment rate for the LAD to which households have moved

Dependent variable takes a value of one if the household moves to a different local authority.

Appendix 4: The main equations of the simulation model

The house price and migration equations are shown in Appendices 1 and 2 respectively.

Table 4.1a: Explaining deprivation (dependent variable = IMD)

Region	Constant	UR	AGE	NOQUAL	ILL	NW	Asian	Black
England	1.860	4.290	−1.188	0.262	1.908	0.136	–	–
England (excluding London)	1.901	3.790	−1.234	0.265	1.992	0.100	–	–
North East	2.609	3.608	−0.270*	0.323*	2.062	1.370	–	–
North West	3.373	5.297	−1.601	0.161*	2.034	0.368	–	–
Yorks & Humber	3.769	3.017	−1.205	0.454	1.781	0.352	–	–
East Midlands	2.332	6.190	−0.371*	0.208*	1.272	1.143	–	–
West Midlands	5.903	4.267	−0.818	0.113*	1.957	0.192*	–	–
East	0.457	4.511	−1.047	0.369	1.660	0.108*	–	–
Greater London	0.281	5.611	−2.080	0.871	0.634*	0.019*	–	–
South East	0.733	3.451	−1.312	0.273	2.064	0.114	–	–
South West	0.208	4.044	−0.928	0.272	2.029	0.336*	–	–
England	1.850	4.062	−1.204	0.280	1.930	–	0.099	0.281

Key:

IMD	=	Index of Multiple Deprivation
UR	=	% of the population aged 16-74 who are unemployed
AGE	=	% of the population aged 16-74 who are retired
NOQUAL	=	% of the population aged 16-74 who have no qualifications
ILL	=	% of the population with limiting long-term illness
NW	=	% of the population who are Black or Asian
Asian	=	% of the population who are Asian or Asian-British
Black	=	% of the population who are Black or Black-British

All variables are measured relative to regional averages

* denotes insignificantly different from 0 at the 5% level.

Table 4.2a: Employment and unemployment (all variables are in logs)

	const	% Black	No- qual	Qual1	% POP 16–24	% POP 25–29	% ILL	% Female	R²	SEE
Full time (FT)	−0.014 (5.37)	0.004 (1.47)	−0.084 (3.40)	0.208 (11.07)	−0.257 (14.78)	0.265 (15.12)	−0.266 (12.65)	−1.079 (6.59)	0.843	0.035
Part time (PT)	−0.038 (9.36)	−0.013 (3.23)	−0.105 (2.76)	0.201 (6.91)	−0.058 (2.16)	−0.249 (9.16)	−0.109 (3.33)	1.004 (3.96)	0.694	0.055
Unem- ployment (UR)	0.017 (1.74)	0.063 (6.67)	0.410 (4.45)	−0.254 (3.61)	−0.027 (0.42)	0.362 (5.51)	0.867 (10.96)	0.612 (0.99)	0.787	0.133

Key:

UR	=	% of the population aged 16-74 who are unemployed
PT	=	% of the population aged 16-74 who are employed part time
FT	=	% of the population aged 16-74 who are employed full time
No-qual	=	% of population with no qualifications
Qual1	=	% of population with level 1 qualifications
% POP 16-24	=	% of population aged 16-24
% POP 25-29	=	% of population aged 25-29
% ILL	=	% of the population with limiting long-term illness
% Black	=	% of population who are black.
% Female	=	% of population who are female

The determination of local authority incomes

The income measure is taken from Wilcox (2003)

$$\ln(INC) = -0.0147 + 0.584\ln(FT) - 0.280\ln(PT) - 0.097\ln(UR) + 0.245\ln(QUAL45)$$
$$\quad\quad\quad (1.9) \quad\quad (6.2) \quad\quad\quad\quad (3.6) \quad\quad\quad\quad (2.6) \quad\quad\quad\quad (9.3)$$

$$(3)$$

t-values in brackets

$R^2 = 0.52$
Equation standard error = 0.117
INC = average local authority incomes
QUAL45 = % of population with Level Four/Five (degree) qualifications
Other terms are defined earlier in this appendix.

Appendix 5: Details of the case studies

Case study participants

Werrington, Peterborough

Interviewees

- Peterborough City Council Housing Strategy Manager – Housing Needs
- Peterborough City Council Community Regeneration Officer
- Peterborough City Council Principal Research and Information Officer, Planning Services
- Neighbourhood Manager, Werrington Cross Keys Homes
- Head of Housing Cross Keys Homes
- Head of Strategy Cross Keys Homes

Resident focus group

Werrington Neighbourhood Council meeting:
- Six males, four females
- Three city councillors
- Seven neighbourhood council members (one elected)

Meeting, individually and in groups, with tenants of Loxley Sheltered Housing Complex, Cross Keys Homes

Newbiggin Hall, Newcastle

Interviewees

- Chief Executive, Nomad Housing
- Assistant Chief Executive, Nomad Housing
- Community Housing Manager, Your Homes Newcastle
- Tenant Involvement Officer, Your Homes Newcastle
- Manager in Market Renewal Pathfinder, Newcastle City Council (Former Housing Renewal Officer and Manager of SRB funded North West Partnership)
- Housing Renewal Manager (Private), Newcastle City Council (Former coordinator of SRB4 Programme, North West Partnership)

Resident focus group

- Five local residents took part in a focus group arranged by a Nomad Housing representative:
- Four females, one male
- One owner-occupier
- Four tenants – three had lived in Newbiggin Hall since first built

Hulme, Manchester

Interviewees

- Former member of the Council for Economic Development in Hulme Regeneration and of City Challenge in Manchester
- Former Community Leader, Hulme
- Housing Officer, Hulme, The Guinness Trust
- Senior European Officer North West Network (Former Chair of Manchester and Hulme Economic Regeneration Forum and Executive Director Firmstart – Economic Development in Hulme)

Resident focus group

- A pre-arranged focus group was cancelled due to lack of sufficient response from residents. It is key to note that a number of research projects were ongoing in Hulme concurrently and residents understandably noted concern of over-consultation. Key contacts who were instrumental in arranging meetings were clearly being consulted by a number of research teams.

Secondary sources

A range of secondary sources were utilised for each of the case study areas including Census data, existing research and local reports. These are fully referenced throughout the text.